I0074020

THE GREAT INHERITANCE

THE GREAT INHERITANCE

7 STEPS TO LEAVING BEHIND
MORE THAN YOUR MONEY

JUSTIN M. BIANCE, CEP®

rescat
PRESS

COPYRIGHT © 2018 JUSTIN M. BIANCE

All rights reserved.

THE GREAT INHERITANCE

7 Steps to Leaving Behind More Than Your Money

ISBN   978-1-5445-0070-6 *Paperback*

978-1-5445-0069-0 *Hardcover*

INVESTMENT ADVISOR DISCLOSURE

Justin Biance is registered as an Investment Advisor Representative and is a licensed insurance agent in the state of Florida and North Carolina. J. Biance Financial is an independent financial services firm that helps individuals create retirement strategies using a variety of investment and insurance products to custom suit their needs and objectives. Investment advisory services are offered only by duly-registered individuals through AE Wealth Management, LLC (AEWM). AEWM and J. Biance Financial are not affiliated companies.

The contents of this book are provided for informational purposes only and are not intended to serve as the basis for any financial decisions. Any tax, legal, or estate planning information is general in nature. It should not be construed as legal or tax advice. Always consult an attorney or tax professional regarding the applicability of this information to your unique situation.

Information presented is believed to be factual and up-to-date, but we do not guarantee its accuracy and it should not be regarded as a complete analysis of the subjects discussed. All expressions of opinion are those of the author as of the date of publication and are subject to change. Content should not be construed as personalized investment advice, nor should it be interpreted as an offer to buy or sell any securities mentioned. A financial advisor should be consulted before implementing any of the strategies presented.

Investing involves risk, including the potential loss of principal. No investment strategy can guarantee a profit or protect against loss in periods of declining values. Any references to protection benefits or guaranteed/lifetime income streams refer only to fixed insurance products, not securities or investment products. Insurance and annuity product guarantees are backed by the financial strength and claims-paying ability of the issuing insurance company.

CONTENTS

ACKNOWLEDGMENTS

Many thanks and appreciation to...

The clients of J. Biance Financial. Your trust and support make working for you an honor.

Michael Loparco, James Bender, and Jill Stouffer for the hours you dedicated to reading and providing feedback on the manuscript.

Rob Livingston, Dr. Bob Schuchts, and Congressman John Rutherford for not only your encouragement and mentorship but also your kind endorsements.

Jason Craig for the time spent whiteboarding, discussing, and editing the content. I know I can always count on two things: your brotherhood and your editing skills.

Annie Carr for your dedication to J. Biance Financial and your motherly care of our clients. Without your hard work, I wouldn't have been able to write this book.

Carol Biance, Michael Biance, and Wendi Peña, you are the biggest cheerleaders in the world; thank you for your constant affirmation of my endeavors.

Jason Biance for being the best friend, business partner, and brother that anyone could ask for, and for writing the foreword.

My children Ava, Monroe, Ellanor, Adelaide, Fulton, Mabel (and Baby Biance #7). It is humbling to be called your father. I am so proud of each of you I could dance on the moon.

My wife, Angela, words cannot express my gratitude. Nothing is possible—or worthwhile—without you, and everything is better when you are involved. Thank you for the late-night proofreading and insightful conversations. I treasure our marriage and love the adventure that is our life together.

And finally, to God for his love and mercy throughout my life and while writing this book. The gift of faith is my Greatest Inheritance.

FOREWORD

———

It was close quarters with my brother growing up. Justin is nineteen months older, we shared a room, and he slept four feet away. My side of the room was adorned with magnificent Florida Gator memorabilia and his with Florida State Seminoles rubbish. When Justin was about thirteen years old, he grew a bit picky about his hair. My theory is that this new emphasis on his grooming had something to do with the girls at school. I don't currently have any evidence to back up this claim, but it is my theory nonetheless.

Whatever the reason, it didn't change the fact that more haircuts meant more money. My mom sacrificed much for our household, which included her three children as well as her two parents. It was a full house and a tall order for a schoolteacher. We never hurt for anything, but money was tight. So when

Justin started asking to get his haircut every eight days, she decided to buy him a set of hair clippers. She said to him, "If you want to have your hair cut that often, you can do it yourself." I was naturally his first victim. Luckily for me, he showed promise early on, and I don't remember any terrible mistakes. In high school, our friends became aware of his new skill set, and Justin would cut their hair from time to time. When he went on to Florida State University, he cut hair for money or beer. My guess is that it was mainly for beer. But again, I currently do not have any evidence to present.

If you have a good relationship with your barber, it makes for great conversation. For me, conversation was great because when Justin cut my hair, I gained insight or another perspective. That hasn't changed for the last twenty-plus years. I'm very grateful for this time and the hundreds of conversations we had. Meetings with my brother are more like meetings with a counselor. He has a lot of wisdom. Although we work in financial planning, his concern with the heart of an issue takes priority. No balance sheet or investment strategy can help issues of the heart; however, within our industry, that is often forgotten or ignored.

I remember leaving the shed one evening (the designated location for cutting hair) after having our forty-seventh conversation about a girl I was dating at the time. I was in my mid-twenties, and Justin had been married for a few years. I said something to the effect of, "I get it this time, and I'm going to have the conversation with her." How he responded was classic. He let out a big, genuine laugh and said, "I hope so, because I've run out of analogies to tell you the same thing again." We both cracked up, because he was right. Justin has always been patient with me, and he is a natural sage. I am completely biased, but Justin's reflective nature, insights, intentionality, and ability to guide someone towards a goal make him a great coach/partner/mentor and a pretty decent barber. I've said it many times: I wish Justin could be everyone's mentor.

I am grateful that Justin has taken the time to write this book. I am excited for you, because now you can get to know Justin, and in a sense, you get to enter his "barber shop." We all need guidance for various aspects of our lives. If we have a knee problem, we go see an orthopedist. If we have an accounting problem, we go see a CPA. If we want to learn the piano, we take lessons from a piano teacher. Why don't most people consult a professional about passing on their life savings? Why don't most people find a professional who knows how to preserve family history and legacy? There is something gravely missing in traditional financial and estate planning, and this book helps fill that void. The steps contained in the following chapters provide a turn-key process for passing on *who you are* along with *what you have.*

As you read, you will find that Justin's education and life experiences make him uniquely suited to help guide your family. Being raised in an intergenerational household and now being married with seven children, Justin understands family life and the importance of preserving unity. We all know that money can complicate that unity.

Justin and I have sat down with hundreds of clients over the years, and we've noticed common desires among them. One of those desires is that, after they leave this earth, their grandchildren will receive a great inheritance, which includes their wealth and their family values. This is a difficult goal in the world today. This book is a roadmap to accomplish that goal.

Life teaches us that anything of worth has responsibility along with it. The wisdom within this book is of great worth; the responsibility is making certain your family benefits from it. This book is not meant to be a good read about an idea. It is not meant to go up on the shelf once finished. Think of it like a recipe. The recipe has to be implemented for us to enjoy a flavorful meal. You will want to share this meal with your family.

Justin is a great mentor, but he is also a challenging one. I encourage you to take the challenge Justin offers in this book. If you do, I am confident you and your family will be blessed for generations to come.

—JASON C. BIANCE
COFOUNDER OF J. BIANCE FINANCIAL

INTRODUCTION

THE MISSING HUMAN EXPERIENCE

Sports were a big part of my childhood. My mom, a single-parent of three children and caregiver to my grandparents, spent most evenings and weekends driving my brother and me to and from practices and games. Baseball was my main sport—my love—but I also played football for a few years in middle school. Back then, you had the starters, the backups, and then the "Taxi Squad," the final string before you get to the fans in the stands. At the end of the game, each team would send out their Taxi Squad to play a fifth quarter. It didn't matter who won the quarter, and the outcome didn't affect the score of the *real* game. The fifth quarter was an opportunity to let these poor kids who had suited up and practiced all week to get a little dirt on their clean jerseys—jerseys they had proudly worn to school that day. I was on the Taxi Squad.

Before the eighth grade, I had never played organized football. Sure, I had played my share of pickup games with the neighborhood kids. My brother and I were always "tackling" each other, throwing one another across whatever room or place we were in (garage, bedroom, dining room, etc.)—but I had never played on a real team. That first year, I didn't play in a real game. Not one game-time minute. I thought I was done with football until the last practice of the year. I am not sure if it was the pent-up energy from not playing all year or the desire to "leave it on the field," but something inside of me changed. I realized that I could throw my body in front of another player (nearly) as hard as I wanted, and my pads protected me. It was exhilarating! It was the best practice I had ever had! And the season was over.

The next year, my freshman year of high school, I played on the freshman football team and continued to improve. By my sophomore year, I was starting strong safety and captain of the junior varsity team. Things were going well. As the season went on, however, I became less and less enthusiastic about practice. There was a lot of conditioning in the Florida heat. Then one afternoon, late in the season, I delivered a tackle that left my shoulder numb. The injury wasn't serious, but my coaches thought I should sit out of practice until I had it checked out. It was my right shoulder, and I remember beginning to worry about what this injury meant for playing baseball. I began to regret ever playing football. My shoulder took a few weeks to heal, and at some point, I decided that going to practice was a waste of time. I quit.

A few weeks later, a varsity coach, Gary Rapp, caught me in the gym and asked me to sit down and have a chat with him. I didn't know Coach Rapp well, but I respected him. He had stopped by the JV practices a few times and had given me some valuable tips on playing safety. When he asked me to sit down, I had a feeling it had to do with quitting the team, but I wasn't sure. Nevertheless, I was nervous. I cautiously sat down, and he said, "I heard you quit." "Yes sir," I responded. "Let me tell you something about quitting, Justin...It's not good. It's not good at all, and the more you do it, the easier it gets." I sat there in silence as those words penetrated my mind. He also sat in silence, making it worse. After what seemed like eternity, the bell rang, I looked up and he nodded as a gesture that our exchange was over. I ran off without saying a word.

Many years later, my eight-year-old son, Monroe,

was playing with a wood building kit we had gotten him for his birthday. It was a simple box with small wood pieces and a manual of designs. The purpose is to build various contraptions, small structures with wood. He was trying to build the hardest design in the manual—of course—but the structure kept collapsing. I watched as his frustration grew with every assembly that fell until finally he yelled, "I quit!" As he sat on the floor with his legs crossed and his head in his hands I said, "You can't quit." He looked up at me, a bit confused and a bit frustrated at what I had said, and responded, "Why not?" I looked at him, smiled, and said, "Because Biances never quit." I watched as a renewed sense of motivation and a sliver of pride filled his spirit. Without saying a word, he began to gather the pieces of wood and attempt to build it again.

As I watched Monroe go back to work, I asked myself, "Where did that come from?" *Biances never quit* was not a family motto; it was not one of many principles that I had written down, a principle I was waiting for the perfect opportunity to communicate to my son. Then suddenly I remembered the conversation in the gym with Coach Rapp. That conversation influenced me more than I had realized. The experience was so formative that it had become a subconscious "rule" that I had lived by ever since. To this day, any time

Monroe and I are working on a difficult project and he notices my frustration, he gently says, "Don't give up, Dad. Biances never quit."

Sharing the principle "Biances never quit" with Monroe was an accident. It was not planned. But it could have been. Life is filled with moments that are formative, but it's getting harder to seize them. These seminal moments turn into *life lessons,* and life lessons turn into *principles and beliefs* that we tend to live by—whether we realize it or not. I am sure Coach Rapp had an experience or two in his life that led him to sit down with me in the gym that day, and now that same principle—*never quit*—resides in the heart of my son.

PASSING ON WHO YOU ARE

While the above experience was not planned, it is quite natural. It is a human experience, which historically, was far more common than it is today. In generations past, the elders of a family saw it as their duty not only to pass on the material wealth that they had accumulated during their lifetime, but more importantly, to pass on the stories and guiding principles of the family. When I talk to clients about leaving a legacy, I am talking about making sure their children inherit *who they are* along with what they have. This includes a family vision that is both connected to past generations and a guide for future generations. Yes, there are always concerns about material wealth, but I find that most retirees—and most people in general—are more concerned with their *family values* and *unity* than they are about their money. Intuitively, they know that unless their family is prepared and unified before they pass away, their wealth will curse more than bless their heirs. The problem is most don't know what to do about it.

There are numerous tools that exist to help you pass on your wealth to your heirs. Perhaps you are concerned about the tax consequences your children might incur at your passing. There are financial strategies to help with that. Perhaps you are worried that one of your children might make poor decisions should he inherit a large sum of money. There are legal instruments to help with that. Maybe you want to set up a fund for your grandchildren's college expenses. There are ways to do that too. Almost every financial, tax, or legal problem you may currently have in your estate can be fixed. As the modern adage goes, "There's an app for that!" Not only do you have countless products and services at your disposal, but there is no shortage of accountants, attorneys, or financial advisors ready and willing to help you. Herein lies the problem. You can have the best investments on the market and the most prominent attorney in the country drafting your trust, but these tools are designed to pass on *what you have*, not *who you are*. This book is written to help you pass on who you are.

James Hughes, a notable estate planning attorney and author, suggests in his book *Family Wealth* that the wealth of a family consists of the family's financial, human, and intellectual capital. He goes on to say, "The family's financial capital is a tool to support the growth of the family's human and intellectual capital."[1] The knowledge and wisdom you have accumulated throughout your life has value. Don't discard it, and don't forget it's yours to pass on, just like your wealth. The hard-earned life lessons you have experienced are the true wealth that your great-grandchildren need to inherit. The question remains, however: Will they? How? When? Where?

PREPARING HEIRS

If we believe there is a need to pass on this personal legacy along with personal wealth, then we should acknowledge most estate planning is missing the most important step. The first part is *Financial Planning*, which protects and grows your money for your

---

1   James Hughes, *Family Wealth* (New Jersey: Bloomberg Press, 2004).

family (hopefully, tax-efficiently). The second part is *Estate Planning,* which plans for the transfer of your money to your heirs. Finally, the third part, which is what many of us miss, is preparing your family for their inheritance. It is essential to pass on not only what you have, but also who you are. If you are not intentional about mentoring your heirs and preparing them for their inheritance, what should have been a blessing could turn into a devastating blow to your long-term family wealth and unity. In such a case, it's not that wealth "ruined" them—did it ruin you?—but that they were not prepared to handle the wealth.

My brother and I have witnessed first-hand the problems that arise when clients do not pass on who they are along with what they have. To me, it's understandable. What do you think of when you hear the word *inheritance*? When I hear the word inheritance, the next word that comes to mind is the word *gift*. If I am going to give a gift, why do I need to prepare the recipient? This is a valid question. Recently my wife, Angela, purchased a doll for one of our daughters. Not any doll, but perhaps the 199th doll in our home. Did my daughter need to be prepared for that gift? Most likely not (except for maybe finding a spot in her room for it). Now, contrast that gift to the first pocketknife I gave to my son. Does he need to be prepared to receive that gift? Yes. *The more serious the gift, the more responsibility comes along with it.* And not only responsibility on the part of the recipient, but also responsibility on the part of the *giver*. If I give my son a pocketknife, something that can be a weapon or a tool, not only does he have to be prepared to receive it, but I have a unique responsibility for his training as a giver and as a father. If I fail to prepare him, what should have been a gift that will bring adventure, activity, and enjoyment to his life might instead be a vehicle for spoil and pain.

You have a similar role to play with your children regarding inheritance. Handing on a vision for your family that is wrapped in your unique story and experience can have an impact for generations. An inheritance is a gift—a gift that requires your heirs to be prepared.

Once, I was sitting down with Susan, a new client, and while reviewing her portfolio she began to tell me about her father. He was a good man who had worked from sun up to sun down his entire life as a farmer in rural central Florida. He had saved well, and at his death, his son and daughter inherited his sizeable estate. Susan, his daughter, was named successor trustee, and she had been in court with her brother ever since the death of her father. She was doing the best she could to carry out her father's wishes, but her brother doubted her intentions and had brought multiple lawsuits. In tears, she shared with me that it broke her heart to see the money her father had worked so hard to earn wasted on attorneys representing feuding siblings. This instance of wealth transition had severed a family in two. What went wrong? What preparation was missing? The father didn't sit down with his children and share the family vision. They didn't gather together at the dinner table and ask, "What mission could we pursue together as a family?" He didn't directly disclose to his heirs the details of his estate and who would lead the transfer process. Communication was sparse, and the family was not prepared.

SHIRTSLEEVES TO SHIRTSLEEVES IN THREE GENERATIONS

You, like me, probably know plenty of other stories of families falling apart after a death because of money. Successfully transferring wealth to heirs has been a problem for millennia. How bad is it? Referring to multiple studies on the transfer of wealth, Richard Beckard—a former professor at MIT—and Gibb Dyer, show that family wealth transitions have a failure rate of 70 percent.[2] The "failure" is when family

---

2   Richard Beckhard, W. Gibb Dyer, "Managing Continuity in the Family-Owned Business" *Organizational Dynamics* 12, no. 1 (Summer 1983): 5.

wealth was lost when transferred from Generation 1 to Generation 2. In other words, what they wanted to do (transfer wealth) didn't happen—it was like dumping a collected bucket of water into open hands.

Over two centuries ago, Adam Smith wrote in *The Wealth of Nations* that, "Riches, in spite of the most violent regulations of law to prevent their dissipation, very seldom remain long in the same family."[3] While Adam Smith was a Scottish economist and moral philosopher, his insight was not revolutionary, and it was not specific to young America. One of the oldest (some say over 2000 years old) and best known Chinese proverbs on the transfer of wealth is 富不过三代 (fu bu guo san dai) "Wealth does not pass three generations." Almost every country on the globe has a similar saying.[4]

"Clogs to clogs in three generations."
—ENGLAND, 1300S

"First generation Trader, second generation Gentlemen, third generation Beggar."
—SPAIN, 1500S

---

3   Adam Smith, *The Wealth of Nations* (London: W. Strahan and T. Cadell, 1776).

4   Perry L. Cochell and Rodney C. Zeeb, *Beating the Midas Curse* (Heritage Institute Press, 2005).

"Seldom three descent continue good."
—GERMANY, 1700S

"Shirtsleeves to shirtsleeves in three generations."
—UNITED STATES OF AMERICA, 1800S

*"From the stables to the stars to the
stables in three generations."*
—BRAZIL, 1900S

Research conducted on families where "new" wealth is generated into the family and then passed on is even more staggering. The same 70 percent rule held true for the transfer from Generation 1 to Generation 2 however, the failure rate of transferring wealth from Generation 2 to Generation 3 was 90 percent.[5] Think about that for a moment. If you are a grandparent, per this research, you have a 10 percent chance of the wealth you have accumulated making its way to your grandchildren. Remember my client who is in litigation with her brother? There is a reasonable chance her children will not receive much of their grandfather's estate.

With a 70 percent (or 90 percent) failure rate for wealth transitions, you may be wondering, what is going on? What is the secret ingredient to making

---

5   Missy Sullivan, "Lost Inheritances," *Wall Street Journal*, March 7, 2013.

sure that my legacy will last multiple generations? As I have mentioned, successful wealth transitions have a lot to do with passing on *who you are* along with *what you have.* I argue that if you are passing on your life story, beliefs, and principles along with your money, you will find yourself in the group of 30 percent success stories.

It is important to review this research while understanding that money is a means not an end. Yes, success rates of wealth transitions get more attention than the success rates of family unity, but our goal is to leave an inheritance that is *far greater* than money. When we analyze the failure rate of wealth transitions, what we are really analyzing is the symptom of a deeper, more important issue. There isn't much research on the "why" behind the failure rate of wealth transfers, but there is one study that is quite fascinating.

Over a twenty-six-year period, from 1975-2001, The Williams Group interviewed 3,250 families that transitioned their wealth. For every 1000 families interviewed, they found the same 70 percent/30 percent success/failure rate.[6] Once again, the success or failure of the transition focused on several

6   Roy Williams and Vic Preisser, *Preparing Heirs* (San Francisco: Robert Reed Publishers, 2010).

questions determining whether family wealth *and* unity endured the transition.

In summary, The Williams Group study found that the families interviewed shared three main causes of wealth transfer failure:

- 60 percent: Trust and communication breakdown within the family unit
- 25 percent: Inadequately prepared heirs (healthy attitudes towards wealth and responsibility)
- 15 percent: All other causes (tax, legal, etc.)

While the macro causes above are related, it is interesting to point out that only 15 percent of the causes for failure were related to the "tools" or services used to prepare the estate. It is common for a retiree to spend much more time with his attorney preparing his estate documents than with his successor trustee preparing him for administration of the trust. *A combined 85 percent of families in the study cited trust, communication, and inadequately prepared heirs as the main culprits undermining successful wealth transfer.* We don't need more precise revocable living trusts, but rather *real trust* in relationships. Heirs need a sense of being a part of an ongoing story, and they need to be prepared to be a part of it. Money, in fact, is a relatively small part of it. Those without great wealth can pass on who they are without money. It seems the real challenge is to pass on who we are with money involved. If you are reading this book, you likely have a unique responsibility and opportunity to ensure that your family wealth and unity lasts for many generations to come. By now you know it's more than assets. It is going to take work—a family vision is not self-perpetuating. *Quality estate documents do not heal relationships and safeguard family bonds.* Refocusing your time to ensure that trust and good communication are regular practices in your family is no small task; neither is creating a family vision and mentoring your heirs so they are prepared to carry your family legacy to future generations. Building this sort of culture takes time, and it is a project that you don't initiate without thoughtful preparation.

BEGINNING THE JOURNEY

You will not be able to prepare your children from the grave or through a trust, so you need to do it now. A friend of mine once told me that being a parent and helping form your children is a *life-long* project. He said that when they become adults, you shift from being a parent to being a life-long mentor—and the real work is only beginning. To this day he, his wife, and their six children produce a quarterly family journal. They all contribute to it, each writing about lessons learned and new topics they feel are important for the larger family. Then once all the articles are gathered, they "publish" the journal and circulate it among the family members. It is a fascinating way for the family unity to remain strong and he and his wife to remain in good communication with their children as they walk with them through their adult life. This family has a clear vision. They have also launched several different family missions. One of their missions was restoring an entire block of a historic city that had fallen to ruin. The project strengthened the family and improved their community. The impact made when a family has a strong vision and mission typically extends beyond the family unit. I suspect, when the patriarch and matriarch of this family pass away, their children will add to and pass on the family vision to their children. When a family vision survives multiple generations, it turns into a *lasting legacy.*

Does your family enjoy this sort of unity? Did you receive this sort of intentional preparation prior to receiving your parents' wealth? Perhaps your parents weren't wealthy, so let me ask this question in another way: Do you know the first name of your great-grandfather? Do you know the defining experiences of his life that made him who he was? Do you know what principles he lived by? Do you know what he believed in? Would you like your great-great-grandchildren to know your story, the principles and beliefs that make you who you are? Most would say yes, but whether it is distance or the busyness of life, most in Generation 1 haven't internalized their story for Generation 2. But you have a choice. You can sit back and hope they pick up worthwhile values and identity from somewhere, or you can be intentional and pass on the value you have. Equipped with the steps contained in this book, you have a tool to help you create the latter.

When our clients begin to consider playing a more active role in creating a family vision, it is common for hesitation to set in. Engaging your children in this way can be a challenging task for a multitude of reasons. Perhaps there has been a divorce in your family and you are not sure how your children would respond. Perhaps you have a child who is estranged from the family. Maybe the thought of "interfering" in your children's busy lives seems like it would be more trouble than it's worth. No family is perfect, and no process is bulletproof. As I write this chapter, it is winter, and I have been spending much of my free time preparing the soil of our garden for the spring. There is a lot of work to be done before my wife, Angela, myself, and our seven children carefully place small seeds in the loose, rich soil. And not only is there a lot of work to be done, but the *preparation* is the *most difficult* work in the process. The first few steps in this process are designed to help you *prepare the soil,* for both you and your children. If proper preparation takes place, you will have a much more fruitful result should you decide to embark on this adventure. Therefore, if you have any of the above hesitations, don't worry: you will be prepared for the journey.

BETTER THAN GOOGLE

We live in an information age; anything we want to know is but a mere internet search away. Or is it? Your life, your story, and your very presence are things that cannot be found on Google. Retirees might be the most undervalued class in society. In a culture that praises production above all other modes of living, it might seem like your worth is synonymous with your work. And now that you are retired, somehow you don't have much to offer. My brother and I are constantly discussing stories that our clients have shared with us. The stories and lessons we have learned from our clients have made us better advisors and better men. You have a lot more to offer your heirs than you realize. And no one else has it.

Your legacy is invaluable, regardless of your portfolio value. Whether your estate is worth millions or thousands, this book is for you. Whether you are widowed, divorced, or have been married for forty years, this book is for you. If you are retired, my hope is that you will leave your children an inheritance that cannot be sold for monetary gain—an inheritance that includes your family DNA. In a word, I hope you leave them a *Great Inheritance.* And when you have left this earth, your children and grandchildren will have a life built on a solid foundation that you helped lay. You will have left behind more than your money; you will have left behind your very self. "The father may die, and yet he is not dead, for he has left behind him one like himself." (Sirach 30:4, Hebrew Proverb)

Step One

CAPTURE YOUR STORY

———

"Every book is a quotation; and every house is a quotation out of all forests, and mines, and stone quarries; and every man is a quotation from all his ancestors."
—RALPH WALDO EMERSON

My wife and I homeschool our children. Yes, she carries out 98.5 percent of the work of homeschooling, but I'm around. She likes to tell the kids that she is the teacher and I am the principle. While I do help if one of the kids is sent to the "principal's office," the other aspect I take part in is the discussion and decision making when it comes to the curriculum and resources we use. The other morning, Angela and I were having a cup of coffee before the children woke, when our conversation turned to family history. We discussed the classic "Family Tree" project that each of us had completed in grammar school; if there is one project that nearly every child in America has done, it is creating a family tree. I remember coming home with this project and having to interview my mom about our ancestors. Angela and I talked about why this is such a common experience and the importance of knowing your family heritage. The conversation was thought-provoking and led to another question: is there any other evidence besides a second-grade project that suggests knowing your family history is important? As we talked, several examples came up.

In 1983, Ancestry, Inc. was founded by a Mormon named John Sittner. The Church of Jesus Christ of Latter-day Saints has always been interested in genealogical research, and they currently own the Family History Library, located in Salt Lake City, which is the largest library for genealogical research in the world. Fueled by his upbringing in the LDS church, John's passion eventually grew to become the online authority in genealogical research. The use of personal computers began to skyrocket in the 1990s, and the genealogists who worked for Ancestry, Inc. began to shift their business towards floppy disks and CD-ROMs. Of course, the internet boom followed, and CDs could no longer hold the amount of data that Ancestry was accumulating. By 2001, Ancestry.

com hit one billion records, and today they have over 2.4 million subscribers in over thirty international markets.[7] Their growth over the last three decades has been phenomenal by anyone's standards, and their annual revenue now exceeds $600 million.

Whether it is the success of this company or our experience building a family tree in grade school, it is safe to say that most people want to know where they come from; most people want to know who their great-great-grandparents were. The home page of Ancestry.com reads, "Discover what makes you uniquely you." The company has even expanded their services into DNA testing. But can the information available on this or any other website really tell you what makes you unique? Can names, photos, and birthdates articulate your family history? Sure, it is neat to learn where your ancestors came from and the family names that have been passed down through generations, but to really know someone, you need more.

I know that my great-grandfather on my dad's side held a prominent position as the president of a railroad and iron ship builder's union in New York. I know his name, his date of birth, and recently, my dad showed me the pocket watch my great-grandfather

---

7   "Our Story," Ancestry.com, accessed January 2018, http://www.ancestry.com/corporate/about-ancestry/our-story.

was given when he retired. All this information is interesting, but I want to know more about my great-grandpa "Pop Biance." I want to know a lot more. What did he think about the culture in the early 1900s? What principles did he live by as the leader of a large organization? What life lessons did he experience that could help me avoid misfortune? There is something about knowing your family story that is powerful, and studies have proven that this knowledge is not merely nostalgic.

THE POWER OF FAMILY HISTORY

Psychologists have pointed out for some time that people who know stories about their relatives have greater emotional stability and maturity. Those who pass on life narratives (stories) that are redemptive, focusing on how good things emerged from bad, show higher levels of emotional well-being and higher levels of generativity—they have more success-positive connection to the next generation.[8] In 2014, a third of adults spent time online learning more about their family history. And the far majority said they benefited from it[9]:

---

8   D. P. McAdams, "The psychology of life stories," *Review of General Psychology* 5, no. 2 (2001): 100-122.

9   "Global Family History Report," Ancestry.com, December 8, 2014, https://blogs.ancestry.com/ancestry/2014/12/08/ancestry-global-family-history-report/.

- 52 percent said they discovered ancestors they had not known about
- 67 percent said that knowing their family history has made them feel wiser as a person
- 72 percent said it helped them be closer to older relatives

Several factors influence an adolescent's emerging identity and well-being as they begin to grow and mature into adulthood. One of those factors is the amount of knowledge they have about their family history. So, not only is it healthy to learn about your family history, but research also shows that it affects your kids as well.

In a study conducted by researchers Dr. Robyn Fivush and Dr. Marshall Duke of Emory University, a system was developed to measure the amount of knowledge an adolescent had about their family story and how it correlated to their well-being. Fivush and Duke created a "Do You Know" (DYK) scale, which consisted of twenty yes/no questions to try to measure adolescents' knowledge of their family history. These questions, given to a diverse group of kids,[10] included things such as how their parents met, or where they grew up and went to school. The youth

---

10 The researchers studied children from 66 middle-class, mixed-race, two-parent families.

were then "scored" in terms of identity development and overall well-being. Although this was a small sample-size, the results were remarkable. The youth who knew more stories about their family history showed "higher levels of emotional well-being, and higher levels of identity achievement."[11]

"There is something powerful about actually knowing these stories," the study said. In the initial research, nine- to twelve-year-old adolescents were the focus group. Several years later, the researchers conducted a follow up study on fourteen- to sixteen-year-old youth and found the same correlation. Interestingly, the older youth who scored high on the "DYK scale" also had a higher sense of self-worth, a stronger ability to plan for the future, an acceptance of one's self, and fewer internalizing and externalizing behavior problems.[12] This follow up study suggested that, while knowing your family story and history is important and formative at a very young age, the benefits do not end as you get older. We have all seen movies where an adult child who never met

---

11 M.P. Duke, A. Lazarus, and R. Fivush, "Knowledge of family history as a clinically useful index of psychological well-being and prognosis: A brief report," *Psychotherapy Theory, Research, Practice, Training* 45, no. 2 (June, 2008): 268-272.

12 Duke Fivush et. al, "Do You Know: The power of family history in adolescent identity and well-being." February 23, 2010, http://ncph.org/wp-content/uploads/2013/12/The-power-of-family-history-in-adolescent-identity.pdf.

their father or mother is restless until they solve the "mystery" of their family history. Whether it is personal experience or documented research, it is safe to say that your family narrative is important. But just because family narrative is important doesn't mean its easy to impart. A variety of factors can diminish our kids' reception of the story.

THE CHALLENGE OF DISTANCE

The technological revolution over the last few decades has dramatically changed the human experience. Some effects have been positive, and others have been crippling. In the history of mankind, we have never had *easier access* to our fellow man, yet we have never been *further from him*. Have you been out to eat lately? The next time you walk into a restaurant, look around. You will find most couples and families sitting across from one another, in each other's *real presence*, but preferring the virtual reality of their smartphone. With phones out and heads down, individuals sit disconnected from the world around them, people included. Access to information and the ability to remain "plugged in" twenty-four hours a day, has made it easier to *know about* someone but harder to *know someone*. Unfortunately, this is one example of how technology has made it more difficult to communicate with our family instead of making it easier.

Like I said, it's not all bad. One of the ways technology has made it easier to communicate is through audiovisual programs that allow loved ones to communicate across continents if needed. I have a friend and client who lives in St. Augustine and regularly has FaceTime with his grandchildren who live in New Jersey, a tool he says he couldn't live without. This ease of communication, however, has also contributed to families being geographically spread out much more than they used to be. Until the last sixty years, most college graduates wouldn't think of applying for a job on the other side of the country, but things have changed.

Most of our clients have children and grandchildren spread out over several states. In a lot of ways, technology has helped these families keep in touch. I remember reading Laura Ingles' *Little House* series with my children and thinking about their trip from their *Little House in the Big Woods* in Wisconsin to their *Little House on the Prairie* in Kansas. When they left Wisconsin, communication with their extended family ended; Laura's grandparents didn't know if they survived the journey. Technology has made it easier to keep in touch across state lines and even countries, but the distance between loved ones in today's world poses new challenges.

Prior to the industrial revolution, families lived near one another, usually in the same towns and often on the same land. Living in close proximity to your family members, both immediate and extended, provides a natural environment for storytelling. I know some families who have a long-standing tradition of Sunday Night Dinner, a time when all the generations gather for a weekly meal. While it is no guarantee, living near your children and grandchildren makes it easier to share your story. In this poem written by Richard Rolle in the early 1300s, you can hear his sense of connection to his ancestors:

> The limbs that move, the eyes that see,
>   These are not entirely me;
>   Dead men and women helped to shape
>   The mold which I do not escape;
>
> The words I speak, my written line,
>   These are not uniquely mine.
>   For in my heart and in my will
>   Old ancestors are warring still.
>
> Celt, Roman, Saxon, and all the dead
>   From whose rich blood my veins are fed,
>   In aspect, gesture, voices, tone,
>   Flesh of my flesh, bone of my bone;

In fields they tilled I plough the sod,
  I walk the mountain paths they trod;
  And round my daily steps arise
  The good and bad of those I comprise.

Did you notice the last stanza of the poem, "*In fields they tilled I plough the sod, I walk the mountain paths they trod...*"? Rolle walks in the fields and works the land his ancestors worked. His connection to them is not only found in his physical features but also in a place, a place that is part of a bigger story. Land used to be one of the most common aspects of a family's heritage; ancestral acres would tie the generations together. While some families, typically those involved in agriculture, may still experience some of this, most do not, because we are no longer an agrarian nation. Perhaps your children and grandchildren are spread out all over the country and you are wondering how you can communicate your family narrative despite the distance.

If your family does not live nearby, it *will* be more difficult, but it is not impossible. In a word, you must be intentional. In the global world that we live in today, if you are not intentional about passing on your family story, it simply won't happen. Geographical distance and family relationships (covered in Step Two: *Restore and Strengthen Family Bonds*) are perhaps the two biggest obstacles to passing on your story. If you want to leave behind more than your money, a good place to start is being intentional about memorializing your family narrative.

THE CYCLE OF NON-COMMUNICATION

In the first chapter, I mentioned several times the importance of having a *family vision*—a guide that can help shape your family's character for generations. In a sense, this means knowing the *characteristics* of what you want your family to look like. As an entrepreneur, I have never been short on vision. Sometimes at night, after the kids are asleep, I'll look up from a book at my wife and say, "You know, [pause] I have been thinking..." to which her response is often, "Oh no." Whether it is a project for our little farm or starting an investment advisory practice, I have no problem in the vision department. Having a vision, however, is the easy part. Casting and implementing a vision is the hard part. We've been talking about how important it is to remember your family story, but we need to make sure that we actually pass it on.

Let's say you have a vision for your family but you haven't been encouraged to bring the potential into actuality. I find that many retirees are more aware of how their children and/or grandchildren *are not* living out their vision than how they *are* living it. Don't get me wrong—I know many parents and grandparents that could dance on the moon they are so proud of their children and grandchildren. I just don't think it is as easy to articulate a clear family vision as it is to point out how things might be going awry. For example, I have a client—we will call him Bill—who is a successful businessman but has struggled for years with the relationship with his adult son. Unfortunately, his son has been in and out of jail due to drugs and many other issues. If I asked Bill whether his son is living within his vision for his family, he would quickly say, "Absolutely not," and point to the various ways, such as drug abuse, that his son is falling short. On the other hand, if I asked him, "Bill, what is your vision for your family?" he may not be able to respond as clearly or quickly. His son may not be reaching for much, but if he has no idea of a family vision, then he has nothing to actually reach for. You can see how a failure to strengthen intergenerational communication creates a sad cycle. Because Bill's son did not receive a story, he's not likely to pass one on.

THE CHALLENGE OF REMEMBERING

Remember, just as your children and grandchildren

are not Adam and Eve, neither are you the beginning of the story. It's time to write down the narrative that you are a part of, because you and your succeeding generations are a part of it. They need to know it. You need to remember it. Life sure speeds up at times, but right now—considering things such as death and inheritance—it's time to do the hard work of slowing down and remembering. Without this remembering, there will be nothing to give.

All parents, myself included, like to teach lessons to our children. Unfortunately, we often miss the most effective way to teach a lesson. If you have a lesson you would like passed on, the most effective means of communicating that lesson is *telling the story behind the lesson learned.* For example, it is easy to say, "Son, there are no shortcuts in life," but it is more difficult and takes more humility to say, "Son, let me tell you about when I tried to take the easy way out of a situation and almost lost everything." You are a repository of know-how earned from trial, hardship, and simply living life. Your children and grandchildren need to learn these lessons. Yes, they will learn their own lessons in life, but you can give them a great head start if you deliver these lessons through story telling.

Recently, I was visiting my ninety-two-year-old

grandmother. We were having small talk, and somehow our conversation turned to when her, my grandfather, and their three children moved from Albany, New York, to south Florida. She explained that they had moved south because my grandfather secured a job with a relative who owned a car dealership. It was a big move. A new place, new job, new apartment, and practically no friends or family for a thousand miles. After a few months in Florida, my grandpa learned that the owner of the company was "cooking the books," as my grandma put it. He was cheating on his taxes and lying to his staff and customers. What did my grandpa do? He resigned. She fed the kids tomato sandwiches because money was so tight. In fact, at dinnertime, grandpa would often not eat because there wasn't enough food to go around.

What did I learn about my grandpa from this story? I learned that he was an honest man. He was a man that wasn't willing to sacrifice his integrity no matter how difficult it might be. I know that he was a man of faith, but this story is evidence of that. Even with a wife and three kids at home, he trusted that his Father in heaven would give him his daily bread. In a word, this story taught me that he was a man of virtue. I was not able to record this story, but at other times, I have pulled out my phone and recorded my grandma as she spoke. If you are technologically inclined, I encourage you to audio or video record as much as you can.

I know that for some of you this might be a big blank. Perhaps you are totally disconnected from previous generations, or maybe there are some characters in the story better left forgotten. This might be a redeeming moment. You might be surprised at how many characters make up the plot of the story, and it might be time for you to do some digging and learn about them and, in the process, about yourself. I can't promise it will be easy or lead to happy endings (my grandpa's virtue, by the way, was not perfection), but I can still confidently encourage you to dig a bit.

To help get you started, below is a list of questions that you can use to reflect and record stories your parents and grandparents might have told you, as well as to document your own stories:

Where were your parents/grandparents born?

What town(s) did they grow up in/live? What family moves led to you being where you are today?

What are some life experiences that your parents/

grandparents had that significantly affected the family?

Write down one word that summarizes your grandparents and great-grandparents. Then record a story you remember that supports that word choice.

What other defining stories did your parents/ grandparents like telling that you would like future generations to know?

What family traditions did you inherit from your parents/grandparents that you would like to see continued?

Was there a hardship that your ancestors endured that you have learned from?

(If married) How did you and your spouse meet? How did you know your spouse was the one to marry?

As an adult, did you have any close friends who you've kept in touch with? Think about the friends who influenced your life and why they were important to you.

Name one thing about each of your kids (if you have them) that stuck out to you as they were growing up.

Name something about raising children that changed from your first child to your last.

How do you want your family and friends to remember you? Of all the ways people could describe you, what words or thoughts would you like to leave with them?

What are you most proud of in your life? Any relationship or professional achievements?

How has your faith or spirituality changed throughout your life? Where did you start, and where are you now?

Was there any experience or event in your life that you didn't think you would make it through? How did you persevere, and what did that experience teach you?

What is the kindest thing you've done for someone else?

This is not an exhaustive list, but hopefully it will help get the wheels turning. Remember, don't simply answer the questions, but also record the stories that come to mind when you read the question. These stories are the building blocks for Step Five: *Create a*

Family Charter, so don't skip it. It may also be helpful to invite another person into this process. If you are married, you and your spouse can interview one another to unearth such memories. If you aren't married, perhaps there is a sibling, cousin, or good friend that would enjoy walking through this process with you. This is a project, not a sixty-minute exercise. If you would like help writing a more detailed family history, I recommend purchasing *To Our Children's Children: Preserving family histories for generations to come*, by Bob Greene and D.G. Fulford. This is a very thorough book that asks you questions about your life, beginning with your childhood to the present day.

LESSONS LEARNED

I don't like to drive, especially at night. When we take family trips, we leave at 3 a.m. I am more awake in the morning, and I like to watch the sun come up. It is also nice that by the time the young kids wake up we have nearly arrived at our destination. One night several years ago, Angela and I had to make a very long drive. My great Aunt Betty had passed away. I could fill this book with the stories that people told at her wake. Many loved Aunt Betty. Missing her funeral was out of the question, but we had to drive at night to make it down in time. I asked Angela if she was up for reading a book aloud to help keep me awake, and she agreed. It was a book that a dear friend and mentor of mine had given me, entitled: *The Total Money Makeover: A proven plan for financial fitness,* by Dave Ramsey. I was a financial advisor helping people every day with their financial decisions and I had never heard of him, which made me initially skeptical. How could something of value in my industry slip by my radar?

We read half of the book on our way down and half of the book on the way back. Let's just say, after reading the book we were sold. We realized we were broke. Between a brand-new car payment, a $2,600/month mortgage, credit card debt, family debt, and student loans, we were broke. The concepts and examples in Dave's book taught us several lessons, such as what you can afford is not what payment you can make, or what great interest rate you can get, or what great credit score you have. No, what you can afford is what you can buy with cash. Reading this book was one of those paradigm-shifting experiences that made us see the world differently.

When we got home, we immediately put our home (also known as our Dream Home, half a mile from St. Augustine Beach) on the market and began selling everything we owned that had value. As chance would have it, we had just bought a brand-new van with all the bells and whistles. I called a gentleman I had worked with in the past who had a retirement gig of helping people buy and sell cars for a flat fee. As I remember the initial conversation, it was quite funny.

"Hi Dan, it's Justin Biance. You helped me buy that Camry a few years back."

"Oh yes, Justin, how are you?"

"I am doing great. I am calling because I would like to sell my minivan and find something else."

"No problem, how old is your minivan?"

"Six months old," I said.

"Did you say six months old?"

"Yes, it's a long story, but I want to sell this van for what I owe and then find something for $4,000 cash."

"That's an interesting request, Justin, let me see what I can do."

Dan called me back about a week later and gave me some good news. He said there was a man who was looking for a new Toyota Sienna XLE with around 5,000 miles on it, but he thought I was asking a little too much. He then said, "I explained to him that you had read some book by a guy named Ramsey and you are trying to get out of a car note. After I said that, his tone completely changed. He asked me what you were going to do if you sold the van, and I told him you were looking for an older minivan and you had $4,000 cash to spend. He paused and softly chuckled. Then he said, tell him he has a deal if he will meet me for lunch." We met at a Cracker Barrel a week later, and he shared his story with me about how living the principles in Dave Ramsey's book made him a millionaire. He also had a Mercury Villager that was twelve years old but was in like-new condition and only had 75,000 miles on it. He bought my van for what I was asking and sold me his van for $4,000 ($1,000 less than its value). This experience taught me a lot, and there are several other stories like it that followed. We sold our house and got serious about getting out of debt. Two and a half years later, we were debt free.

Like any parent, I hope my children are good with money. I hope they don't get into debt, I hope they tithe, and I hope they view money as a *means* not an *end* in their life. How can I help make sure that happens? Well, I could just tell them, "Don't spend money you don't have!" Or, "Live within your means." I could also give them the Dave Ramsey book that helped Angela and me clean up our financial life. However, the best thing I can do is tell them the story I just told you—details included. I look forward to telling them this story. I look forward to sharing all the details, such as the embarrassment of pulling up to church one Sunday in a brand-new van and the next Sunday in a tin can. These are the stories your children and grandchildren need to hear. Learning life lessons is no easy process. As a good friend of mine says, "Failure is compost," because growth comes from compost, but compost often comes from failed crops and scraps. If you capture the stories of your successes *and your defeats,* they will serve as "compost" for many generations to come. You are a reservoir of lessons learned; share them through your story and the stories of those who have come before you.

Step Two

RESTORE AND STRENGTHEN FAMILY BONDS

———

"Forgiveness is the giving, and so the receiving, of life."
—GEORGE MACDONALD

What word comes to mind when you think about your family? Not your current, immediate family, but rather the family you grew up with—your parents and siblings. Is it "love" or "happiness"? Maybe it's "challenged," "broken," or "dysfunctional"? There is one thing that all families share regardless of background or socio-economic status: all families are *different*. That is the word that describes my family growing up; it was most certainly different.

My parents met on a blind date in 1971. My dad was a teacher in Dade County, Florida, and my mom a teacher in Broward County. Mutual friends introduced them, and as my mom puts it, "After the first date, I knew I would marry him—or someone like him—because he came from a good family. He was Italian, and he was Catholic!" A little over a year later, they married. They had three children: my sister Wendi, me, and then my brother. Then, in 1986, we moved from Hollywood, Florida, to Sebring, Florida, when my dad took a position at the Highlands County School Board as Associate Superintendent of Schools. While my mom missed our extended family—who were all still back in south Florida—she knew Sebring would be a good town for raising children. Everything seemed to be going the way it was supposed to. But just as we were feeling settled in our newly-built home, the unexpected happened. My parents divorced.

I was only seven at the time, but I have intense memories of it. I remember the sadness that came over my mom after dad left. I remember our big home feeling very empty. Whether it is divorce, death, or some other fracture, division in a family *changes things*. Our life had changed, and it had become more challenging, but I don't think anyone expected how things would continue to change over the next several years.

Divorce was not foreign to my mom. She also came from a broken home. At the time of my parents' divorce, my mother's father, Grandpa Carta, needed a place to live. He was a retired carpenter, and shortly after my dad left, he was looking for a change of scenery. He was a very active retiree, attending every social the Elks Lodge hosted—if there was dancing. Sebring looked like a good retirement town, and he thought he might be able to help around the house if he came to live with us. My mom agreed. She also knew that, with him nearby, she could care for him as he aged. Our house had two guest bedrooms, so it was a simple decision, and grandpa moved in. Having grandpa there made the house feel a little less empty. Grandpa fixed things at home by day and went out dancing at night. This was good, but it gets better.

During my parents' divorce and the various transitions that came along with it, my mom's mom, Grandma Carta, was caring for her mom, my Noona (Italian for Grandma). In the Italian culture, when you reach the age that you need care, you move into a very special "Assisted Living Facility" commonly called *your children's home*. The Italian culture on my mom's side of the family had a rich bond. If you were *in* the family you were *in*, and if you were *out*, you were *out*. It was so strong that when my great-grandpa Scirpo (Nonno) wanted to move from

Connecticut to Florida when he retired, he built a house for each one of his six children on the same street so they would move down with him.

Two years after my parents' divorce, my Noona passed away. With my great-grandma gone, my Grandma Carta did not want to live alone and knew that she would eventually need care as well. And, well, we had one more open room. Yep, grandma moved in with us. She moved in with her daughter, three grandchildren, and my grandpa, who was also her ex-husband of twenty-five years.

Just to review: after my parents divorced, I lived with both of my divorced grandparents. Remember, I said the situation was "different." Even with the uniqueness, it was still a time rich with experience. Grandma and grandpa were cordial to one another and rarely argued. My grandma was an avid reader and was very cognizant of the world around her. Her physical health, on the other hand, was very poor. She had severe osteoporosis and had to use a walker. Despite her health challenges, she spent most of her days walking to and from the laundry room to help my mom with the piles of dirty clothes her grandchildren produced. She would fill the laundry basket with clean clothes and wedge it inside the legs of the walker (which had tennis balls on the bottom for smooth operation) to bring it to were she would fold it. Thanks to grandma, we always had clean clothes.

Grandpa was in great health physically, but his mind diminished earlier than my grandma's. He was out on the town every day—breakfast with his group downtown at *Dee's Place*, helping at the local St. Vincent de Paul store, or on a date with a "lady-friend." Our weird situation didn't stop his social life. When grandpa was going somewhere, he would yell across the house to my grandma, "If anyone calls, just tell them I'm out." My grandma would look up and roll her eyes as he headed out the door. My favorite exchanges, though, were usually at dinner when they would argue unintentionally. Neither could hear very well. One time, my grandpa was telling a story about his day and in mid-sentence said, "Would you please pass the salt?" to which my grandma looked up and said, "You think that was my fault?" and an argument ensued. Most exchanges were quite entertaining for my siblings and me. The best ones would begin in English and end in Italian. My mom instructed me to never repeat those particular Italian words.

THE VITAL LINK

There are numerous stories that I could share from my childhood—special memories that I cherish thanks to grandma and grandpa living in our home. Whether it was my grandpa teaching me how to drive or sitting with my grandma in her big recliner, there was something special about being connected to them. I am grateful for those memories. *I am grateful because two generations of divorce could have prevented such moments.* My grandparents "left their mark" on my sister, my brother, and me. As I have reflected on their presence in our lives, I realize a combination of factors made that possible. I was raised, in part, by my grandparents, so at first glance that may seem the obvious reason their influence was possible. Looking deeper, however, I realize there was something more vital still. The most important factor allowing my grandparents to pass on *who they were* to me and my siblings was their relationship with my mom. Without this vital link—my grandparents' relationship with my mom—their connection to future generations would have ended with their passing.

My parents are still living, and they have ten grandchildren (and counting). There are very few things that bring them (Generation 1) more joy than their grandchildren (Generation 3). Second only to being married to my wife, Angela, the experience of being a father of seven children has been the greatest blessing of my life. And while they have been a blessing to my wife and me, our parents have a love for them that is hard to describe. My parents well up with joy, pride, and excitement when they see their grandchildren. Our children know at Christmas they get three simple gifts from us. "If three gifts were enough for Jesus," we tell them, "it is enough for you." They don't mind, probably because they know that when grandma shows up for Christmas her back seat and trunk will be filled with wrapped presents. As my mom's financial advisor, I have thought about broaching the subject of how much she spends at Christmas. But it would be pointless.

Watching grandparents love grandchildren is beautiful. Even my clients, who are also part of Generation 1, expect that at meetings the first item for review will be recent pictures of my kids. While the love that exists between Generation 1 and Generation 3 is remarkable, it is not the most vital for the long-term unity of your family. Am I saying turn the dial down on your love for your grandchildren? I wouldn't dare. That is like telling my mom to stop giving Christmas gifts to my children. What I am saying, though, is if you "skip over" your relationship with your children, your long-term family legacy and unity could be in jeopardy.

There are several family principles that my siblings and I "caught" from our grandparents. Yes, it was easy to have a relationship with them because they lived in our home and helped raise us. But what if they hadn't? What if the conflict from my grandparents' divorce severed their relationship with my mom and they never moved in? What if my grandparents and my mom had some long-standing unresolved conflict? Was my mom's relationship with my grandparents perfect? Far from it. Can you imagine living with and caring for your two divorced and elderly parents? No, their relationship was not perfect, but it did provide for our family to maintain intergenerational relationships. The "vital link" between my mom and her parents connected us to them. If that link would have been broken, my grandparents' legacy would have died with them.

YOUR WITNESS REMAINS

Over the last five to ten years, the way we design and structure estates using life insurance reveals a growing disconnect between generations. Utilizing life insurance for leaving tax-free money to heirs is nothing new; however, more non-traditional structures are now becoming more common. For example, Generation 1 creates a multigenerational trust and then funds a life insurance policy owned by the trust. The trust owns the policy, the children (Generation 2) are the insured, and the grandchildren (Generation 3) are the beneficiaries of the policy. While Generation 2 is the insured (the policy is based on their life expectancy), they have no ownership or control over the trust. The policy was created based on Generation 2's life, but that is the only part they play in this plan.

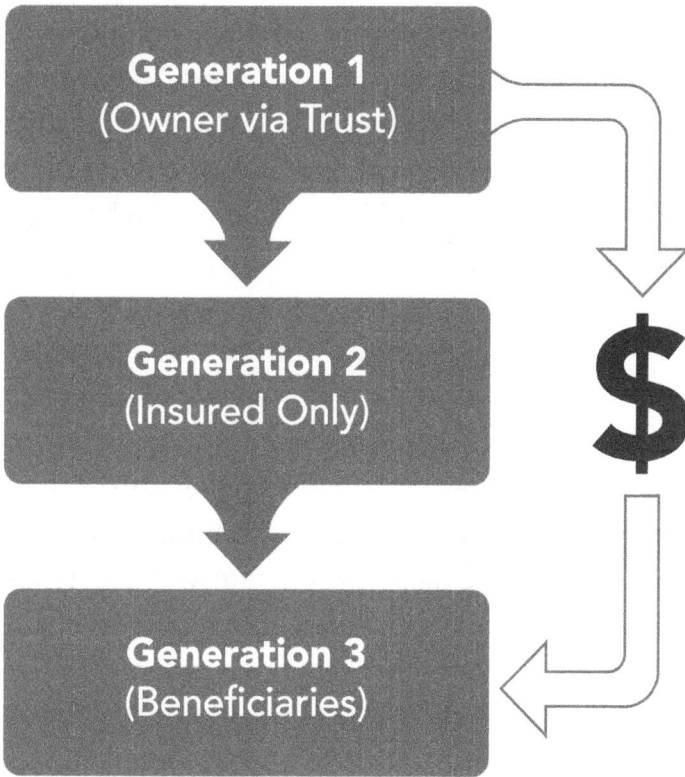

With this design, grandma and grandpa (Generation 1) have successfully left their grandchildren a substantial sum and completely skipped their own children in the process. And since the policy is based on the life of their children (Generation 2), their grandchildren won't receive the proceeds until they are much older—when their parents (Generation 2) pass away—another added benefit, as far as Generation 1 is concerned.

This is one of several ways that "controlling from the grave" is becoming more common. Is there anything wrong with this type of design? Not necessarily; however, if we take a closer look, it could tell us something about the different relationships between generations. Some retirees will use this design, and others to simply earmark and leverage a portion of their estate for their grandchildren. These grandparents are not trying to "cut out" their children; they just want to leave their grandchildren a specific sum, separate from their other assets. Other retirees lack a certain amount of trust in their children and fear that, if they leave their entire estate to them, it may not eventually make it to their grandchildren. A fear validated by centuries of lost fortunes—remember, *"Shirtsleeves to shirtsleeves in three generations."* There are good reasons to be discerning when it comes to planning the eventual transfer of your wealth. I encourage you, however, to spend just as much time on *restoring relationships* during your retirement years as you do planning the distribution of your assets.

This really is a *necessary* step if leaving a Great Inheritance matters to you.

I know grandkids are great, but if you love your grandchildren and great-grandchildren—and you want them to remember you, to tell your stories, and to carry on your legacy to their children—the best thing you can do for them is love their parents (your children). One of the reasons this is so vital is because after you are gone, it is your children who are going to make sure that your grandchildren and great-grandchildren remember you and pass on your story and principles. Your children are the "living image" of you after you leave this earth. Your witness to your grandchildren, through the way you handle your relationship with their parents, will be noticed. That relationship binds the generations together and lays the foundation for generations to come. It's tempting to skip over conflicts with your children and just enjoy the grandkids, but if you want the *legacy* we are talking about, you'll need to give each generation the love that only you can give.

REENGAGING

At this point, you may be wondering, "What does all of this have to do with my money?" Most financial and legal books that cover the topic of inheritance and legacy planning do not spend enough time discussing relational issues. And as I have noted, studies show that relational issues are the main culprit of unsuccessful wealth transfers.[13] Yes, if your financial and legal affairs are in order it may help prevent further conflict for your heirs, but that is not the goal of this book. If you desire to leave your children more than your money, the biggest potential obstacle preventing that is a strained relationship with your children. Is this a fun topic? No. Personally, I have found that reconciliation with anyone is almost always difficult and awkward, but when done well, it is *always fruitful*.

A good starting place for reflection is asking yourself this question: is my relationship with my son/daughter stronger or weaker than it was when they were ten years old? That may seem like a strange question, but it really helps quiet the noise around your current relationship with your children. When your children were in their adolescent years, they were probably a little easier to love. It was after the "terrible twos" and before the teen years. They came to you when they had a question about something, desired your time and approval, and everything about their life was exciting and new. I've experienced this age as a

---

13 Roy Williams and Vic Preisser, *Preparing Heirs* (San Francisco: Robert Reed Publishers, 2010)

lot of fun. Now, I know a parent-child relationship is very different than a parent-adult child relationship, but I think it is important to remember a time when that relationship was somewhat conflict-free. Did you have to raise your voice from time to time to get your children to clean their room or stop fighting? Yes. But this was most likely a special time in the history of your relationship with your children. What has happened since then? Life. And with life comes all kinds of circumstances that can strain any relationship. But we can also strain it. Without some sort of reconciliation, these strains tend to grow and become the defining aspect of the relationship. And, typically, all parties share part of the blame. Regardless of what conflicts may have transpired since your children were young, now is the time to *reengage and restore* the relationship. Will it be a perfect process? No. Will it be as healed and secure as it was when your children were young? No. Perfection is not the goal, and neither is an idealistic (and unrealistic) vision for your family. There is, however, a good reason for you to climb this mountain, and if you take the lead, you could help restore the vital bond between generations.

SPLINTERS & PLANKS

Spiritual leaders and older couples have given my

wife and me indispensable guidance and a living example of what a healthy marriage should look like. We met on a campus ministry retreat in college, meeting several spiritual "sages" along the way. One of those mentors was Dr. Bob Schuchts, a marriage and family counselor (also author of the books *Be Healed* and *Be Transformed*). After I proposed to Angela, I asked Dr. Bob if he would lead our marriage preparation. Over the course of a year, we went through pre-marital counseling and learned a lot about how our families handled conflict growing up. Most importantly, we set up a "structure" or process of how we would handle conflict resolution. Learning how to reconcile so early in our relationship was perhaps the greatest wedding gift we were given. As we now approach our fourteenth year of marriage, I can honestly say that our hearts would be much further apart had we not had this skill and used it hundreds of times throughout our marriage.

During our counseling sessions, there were several "golden nuggets" that made an impact on us and became principles that we would live by. For example, in our home the words "I'm sorry" and "It's okay" aren't allowed. If I have hurt someone, it is not *okay*, but it can be *forgiven*. If an apology is necessary, the words that we use are "Please forgive me" and "I forgive you." It is easy to blow though an attempt to apologize with the words "I'm sorry," but it is more difficult to do that with "Please forgive me." Likewise, it is easy to say "It's okay" and not truly forgive.

Another principle I learned from Dr. Bob was a healthy understanding of the role of a leader in a relationship. I remember sitting in Bob's office when this topic came up. He asked me, "Justin, you and Angela will serve one another in your marriage, and you are equals, but who is the leader?" I thought about the question for a moment and then proudly said, "Scripture says I am the head of the household, so I am." "Very good," Bob commented, "And as the leader of your family, what are your responsibilities?" "Well, to provide for my family and protect them. I suppose that is what good leaders do." "Yes, very good." Bob replied. Then he went on to say, "Justin, there is one other area I would like you to take the lead on in your marriage, and it is a role that most men don't do very well." When he said this, I was a little nervous about what he would say next. He continued, "As the leader of your marriage, I want you to always *initiate* reconciliation."

This was unexpected and a bit confusing. My belief about reconciliation (while never consciously thought about until that day) was that the person who had more fault in a conflict should be the one to initiate reconciliation. Then again, experience had taught me that method only led to neither party initiating, or one of the parties trying to reconcile but also accuse at the same time ("I'm sorry...But you know you had some fault here too.") Bob went on to say,

"Whether you feel your fault in a conflict is 1 percent or 99 percent, as the leader I want you to be the one to initiate 100 percent of the time. I want you to be the first one to find your fault (the plank in your eye, not the splinter) and ask Angela for forgiveness, without expectation of reciprocation."

Wow, I thought, that is a tall order. When Dr. Bob said initiate reconciliation, I had a feeling he *didn't* mean when there is an argument I should go to Angela and say, "Okay this is how you hurt me and I am ready for your apology." And when he handed me a Bible turned to Matthew 7:3—"Why do you observe the splinter in your brother's eye and never notice the great log in your own?"—it became clear what he meant. Trusting Dr. Bob, I listened and implemented what he told me for two reasons: 1) Bob's words felt challenging but good, and I wanted to have a strong marriage, and 2) most of the conflicts are my fault anyway.

I was giving a talk at a men's conference once, and

I shared this challenge to the men in the audience. I was applying the principle to leadership in general. I said that if you are a leader of a team or staff and there is a conflict, as the leader you should *take the lead* and initiate reconciliation. After the conference was over, I was standing with a friend discussing the event. A man walked up to us and asked me if I really believed what I said about leaders initiating reconciliation. I said yes. He went on to tell me that if a leader initiates reconciliation with one of his staff, doesn't that make him look weak and undermine his authority? Before I could answer, my friend spoke up. "I have worked for Justin in the past and he has exercised this principle with me. I can tell you that it made me respect him more. It made me want to follow him more, and it showed me that he was secure in his leadership." I was both speechless and deeply touched.

BE COURAGEOUS

As the matriarch and patriarch of your family, you are the leaders. Until you pass the torch of your family leadership to your heirs, you are the leader. And with this responsibility comes *initiating reconciliation*. Whether you have experienced small conflicts or large ones, initiating reconciliation is your job. There are few things more powerful than someone approaching you and asking forgiveness *with no expectation of reciprocation.*

Imagine that your father or mother is still alive. Imagine one of them coming to your home with an apology, a request for forgiveness with no focus on their own hurt. I remember where I was sitting when my dad called me and initiated reconciliation for the first time in our relationship. I was sitting on the front porch steps of my apartment in college. Was that a powerful experience? I remember which step I was sitting on. Few experiences are more powerful than when a parent asks his child to forgive him.

A few years back, I was tucking my son into bed, and it occurred to me that I needed to ask his forgiveness for yelling at him. I said, "Monroe, please forgive me for yelling at you." To which he responded, "Dad, please forgive me for misbehaving." Did you catch that? He didn't respond with "I forgive you," he responded by focusing on his own fault. If you initiate reconciliation *without expectation of reciprocation,* you can't imagine what the impact of your witness might do. Yes, there may be good reason for your children to ask for your forgiveness, but it is your humility, as the leader of your family, that will break down walls and heal wounds.

Building a culture of unity rather than division in your family is worth the effort. The purpose of this chapter is not a suggestion to hire a therapist and set up a counseling session with your children. Yes, there are counselors, books, and models for handling conflict resolution. The goal of this step is to encourage you to engage your children. More specifically, it is to share with you the influence you have should you approach your children with humility. If you find the plank and initiate reconciliation without expectation of reciprocation, the rest will be easy. I have witnessed people talking in circles for hours trying to resolve a conflict because they don't start there.

Your relationship with your children might be strong, it might be cordial, or it might be on the rocks. Regardless of where on the spectrum your relationship with your children falls, there is always room for improvement. If you have the courage to take Step Two, you are beginning to leave a legacy that few have the courage to leave.

Step Three

DESIGN AN ORDERLY ESTATE

———

"Rule number one: Never lose money. Rule number two: Never forget rule number one."
—WARREN BUFFET

As far as any boy would be concerned, my brother Jason and I grew up in a dream neighborhood. Our large backyard overlooked Lake Josephine, known more for its alligators than for its fish. Beyond the road in front of our house was a large forest with four-wheeler trails and plenty of room for adventure. Every day when we got home from school, we would drop our bags and mom wouldn't see us until dinner. We lived outside. Whether we were whirling axes to cut down trees for forts, playing pick-up games of tackle football with the kids in the neighborhood, or catching alligators off our dock, we loved the wildness of our kingdom on Oak Beach Boulevard.

Now that I have children of my own and I see the risks they take (especially my boys), I often sit back and wonder, "How did I survive childhood?" There is something about being young that makes you feel invincible. That is how Jason and I felt growing up; we had plenty of energy and the imagination and environment to put it to use. There were no guardrails and no limits. We were free to live our boyhood fervently. At least that was our reality when we were *outside.*

Our reality when we were *inside* was quite different. Our grandparents lived with us and helped raise us. Watching the challenges they endured during their retirement was a stark contrast to carefree life outside. We witnessed the daily activities of typical retirees—many of them joyful and pleasant, and others quite difficult. One example I remember clearly is the constant scheduling of doctors' appointments, going to doctors' appointments, and then coming home to schedule next week's doctors' appointments. As my grandma aged, her arthritis became quite severe, making her fingers turn inward. I remember Jason cutting grandma's food at dinner because it was too difficult. Imagine cutting down trees in the woods for a fort and then hours later cutting your grandma's food. Outside was carefree, but inside we learned that life is short and things change. We knew intuitively that the risks we were taking as boys would not continue as we got older. These were formidable moments that we didn't realize were taking place; they were experiences that planted seeds that wouldn't mature for years.

Jason and I ventured in different directions after college and graduate school. Jason became a risk analyst for a large Fortune 500 company, and I helped launch and run two entrepreneurial start-ups. We both enjoyed our work but were unsatisfied. Jason analyzed risk for his company and helped them safely invest millions, but it was unfulfilling. You may know people like this too, but I am always amazed at how good Jason is with people, and how good he is at judging character. In his job, he was helping a company, but he wanted to help people. One December afternoon, we were both home for the holidays and decided to go golfing. We were discussing work, and I cast the idea of starting a financial firm together that specialized in holistically serving retirees. Jason had spent nearly a decade in financial services, and the last company I helped start was a financial firm. Eighteen holes of golf takes about four hours, but our conversation made it feel like we completed the round in thirty minutes. We decided that, after the round, we would fast from discussion on the topic and simply take it to prayer. The next time we spoke, we both felt confirmed in the decision to start a business together.

The seed that was planted growing up with our grandparents, as well as our professional experience of finance and entrepreneurship, all culminated in us starting *J. Biance Financial.* When we laid out our vision for the firm, there were several principles that we believed were important for retirees, and these were heavily influenced by our experience with our grandparents. Our practice is built around these principles, and we strongly believe they are also the backbone of an orderly estate. The last step helped bring people together through reconciling, and this step helps keep things orderly and peaceful so that conflict doesn't come up later.

To take this step, you need to understand *what type of advisor* is best positioned to help you and also *what their priorities should be* in helping you design an orderly estate. I have mentioned that retirees are one of the most undervalued classes in society. They are also one of the most vulnerable. Therefore, the person in whom you put your trust—and their priorities—*will* impact your legacy.

UNDERSTAND YOUR RISK

Thinking back to our young lives of dangerous adventure, I find it ironic that one of the main areas we focus on today in our practice is risk mitigation. When you are young, you feel invincible. As you get older, well, let's just say you are a bit more calculated. Retirees enter a new season in life. Most Americans work nearly 90,000 hours before they retire. Those hours are worked in order to reach a point in life when you can stop working (or at least stop working for a wage) and still have an income. When you reach that point, it is a mixed bag of emotions. You get excited about the idea of traveling, spending more time with the grandkids, or picking up a new hobby, but you are also a bit frightened. Whether you are nearing retirement or in retirement, you may remember the mix of emotions that comes with crossing this threshold. The element of fear that you experience is due to this simple and sobering fact: retirement means you are *permanently unemployed.*

There are differences between temporary unemployment and permanent unemployment, but the very fact that the prospect of future employment is slim should affect your decision making. If managed well, your nest egg will not only provide the income you need during retirement, but it will also bless those you love when you pass away. To manage your life savings well, you must take risk seriously. Time is no longer on your side, so the strategy you employed as you saved for retirement *must change*. If measuring and mitigating risk isn't agenda item number one when you sit down with your financial advisor, it is time to trust someone else with your life savings.

Have you ever walked into a broker's office and one of the first things you do is take a risk tolerance questionnaire? These tests ask you basic questions and then classify you into one of five main buckets based on your answers. Those buckets (Morningstar Risk Classifications) are: Conservative, Moderately Conservative, Moderate, Moderately Aggressive, and Aggressive. It is good to know your risk tolerance, but do you think being tagged one of these five classifications really says anything about how much money you are willing to lose? Let's say there were 100 people in a room all classified as having a Moderate risk tolerance, and their portfolios were all invested based on a Moderate rating. Do you think they would all react *in exactly the same way* if they experienced a stock market correction? Do you think, if they were each asked to "define a devastating loss," they would answer in the same exact way? The five buckets don't say much about your risk tolerance. It's just not specific enough.

In our practice, we use a quantitative tool built on a

Nobel Prize winning behavioral study to determine our client's risk tolerance. This tool, however, doesn't provide one of the five risk ratings above. It assigns a *Risk Number*. That makes sense, doesn't it? For almost every type of analysis in almost every field, we use numbers to measure things. Do you drive too fast? Check your speed (number). Is your cholesterol too high? Check your LDLs and HDLs (number). Did your grandson do well on the SAT? Check his score (number). Yes, we use numbers to quantify almost every area of our life—except in financial services. Isn't that ironic? Whether your advisor uses this or a similar tool to identify your true risk tolerance, don't settle for the five big-tent categories above (Conservative, Moderate, etc.). It's more important now than ever before.

Most financial professionals use words instead of numbers to measure your risk tolerance. Most retirees haven't experienced a portfolio accurately aligned with their goals and concerns. Most retirees have just gotten used to the phrases, "Don't worry, we're in it for the long haul," or, "Don't worry, it's not a real loss; it's just a paper loss," and they don't realize there can be a better way. As you read this book, you will find that leaving behind more than your money takes time and intentionality. It takes focus on what I like to call *first things*: your stories, principles, and beliefs—in summary, your vision for your family. Do you want to devote mind-share to preparing your heirs and leaving a legacy, or would you rather spend your time worrying about your money and riding the Wall Street rollercoaster? If you understand your risk and design a financial strategy that aligns with your risk tolerance, you can sleep well at night knowing if the stock market were to soar into double digit returns or crash, everything would go according to plan—no surprises. If this area of your estate is orderly, it will provide freedom to focus on more important things.

ACCUMULATION VS. DISTRIBUTION

The lifecycle of an investor is divided into two "seasons" or phases: the *Accumulation Phase,* and the *Distribution Phase*. The Accumulation Phase begins when you open your first investment account with the hope of one day retiring. Your goal is to save as much as possible and grow those funds aggressively, because time is on your side and the market, over time, trends upward. This long-term strategy worries less about bursts of volatility, because they pass.

The Distribution Phase begins when you start to near retirement. You have saved well, and it is now time to start planning your income. It is time to plan how you will make the money you *accumulated* over the last thirty to forty years last for the rest of your life. And with life expectancies continuing to lengthen, retirement could last a very long time. Remember when I said that retirement means you are *permanently unemployed*? This is the Distribution Phase. It is possible that you may have to live on your assets just as many years as you spent accumulating them. This type of planning is incredibly important, and it requires a specialist. The needs of a forty-year-old aggressively saving for retirement are very different from a sixty-five-year-old deciding how much of his IRA he should withdraw annually for income.

Are you working with a financial professional that specializes in asset accumulation or asset distribution? Below are ten questions that you can use to determine what type of advisor you might have. In our opinion, you should be able to answer "yes" to all of these questions when working with someone who focuses on distribution:

1. Do you have a detailed distribution plan in place that projects all your streams of income from now until age 100?
2. Do you have a spousal continuation plan in place that details how a surviving spouse will make up lost income due to the first spouse passing?

3. Do you have a summary of assets in place that lists all your assets, the taxable nature of those assets, and who the beneficiary is?
4. Do you know your risk tolerance (more specifically, your *Risk Number*) and the amount you could lose if you experienced a market correction or crash?
5. Has your advisor spoken with your attorney to make sure that you have all your necessary legal documents in place?
6. Does your advisor meet with your CPA or accountant to make sure your estate is structured as tax-efficiently as possible?
7. Has your advisor spoken with you about long-term care? Not necessarily offered you a product to purchase, but asked you what your desires are for your care?
8. Has your advisor offered to meet with your heirs, explain in detail how your estate is structured, and help prepare the person you have appointed to lead the wealth transfer process?
9. Has your advisor classified your assets into the three Tax Buckets (described later in this chapter) and suggested strategies for transferring assets into the Tax-Free Bucket?
10. Does your advisor meet with you at least annually to review the above areas and adjust your plan according to your goals or changes in your life?

This is not a comprehensive list, but it should give you an idea of the type of service you should expect from a distribution specialist. In our practice, we have built a proprietary planning system called the *Sound Retirement Blueprint.* Our process is designed to help ensure that the five key areas of your financial life are in order. They are: income planning, investment planning, tax planning, healthcare planning, and legacy planning. You can probably gather from the list above the types of services we provide. These are the areas your advisor should be helping you with. You should be working with a financial advisor that is uniquely positioned to be a sort of "general contractor" for your entire estate and get it in order. That, however, isn't the only characteristic to look for.

BROKER VS. FIDUCIARY

If you are looking for an advisor who will provide the type of service appropriate for retirees, you should also be looking for a fiduciary. A fiduciary is someone who, by law, *must put your interest above his own.* Attorneys have similar legal requirements as fiduciary advisors. If an attorney fails the attorney-client relationship (which is a breach of fiduciary duty), they could be disbarred. Is the same true for a financial advisor? There are some financial advisors who are fiduciaries, and there are some who are not.

Advisors who are subject to a suitability standard are also called brokers and work for a broker/dealer. Advisors who are subject to a fiduciary standard are called investment advisor representatives and work for a registered investment advisor.

When an aspiring financial advisor begins taking classes and exams for his license, there are two different routes he can take. He can choose a license that holds him to the *fiduciary standard*, or he can choose a license that holds him to a *suitability standard*. If he chooses (or the firm he works for chooses for him) the license that subjects him to the suitability standard, his recommendations to a client must be suitable for the client. Could a recommendation be suitable and not be in the client's best interest? Yes. For example, as an investor, you may have enough liquidity in your portfolio to purchase a variable annuity (the purchase is suitable) but due to high fees and surrender charges, it might be better for the broker selling the variable annuity than it is for you. Does this mean that all brokers are out to do what is in their best interest and not yours? No. However, if you are going to trust someone with your life savings, it is best to trust someone who is held to the fiduciary standard (the very word fiduciary comes from the Latin *fiducia*, which means trust).

Recently, the word fiduciary has been making headlines. There is now legislation that expands the "investment advice fiduciary" definition under the Employee Retirement Income Security Act of 1974 (ERISA). This legislation (1,023 pages in length) would elevate all financial professionals who *work with retirement plans or provide retirement planning advice* to the level of a fiduciary, bound legally and ethically to meet the standards of that status. Those who would be impacted the most by this law are brokers. As explained above, brokers currently operate under a suitability standard, not a fiduciary standard. Another important caveat to point out is that this rule would only subject brokers to act as a fiduciary on *retirement accounts* (IRAs, 401[k]s, etc.). Therefore, they would not be held to the fiduciary standard when managing non-qualified or after-tax money.

CAPTIVE VS. INDEPENDENT

Perhaps you are familiar with this scripture passage: "No one can serve two masters; for either he will hate the one and love the other, or he will be devoted to the one and despise the other."[14] I have found that these words apply to several areas of my life, and one of those is my work with retirees. Financial advisors are either "captive," which generally means they

14 Mat 6:24 RSV

work for a publicly traded company (ex. Edward Jones, Ameriprise, Merrill Lynch) or they work for an independent firm. If I worked for Ameriprise, I would essentially have two bosses: you as my client and my boss at Ameriprise. I would have quotas to make, proprietary products to sell, and at the end of the day, if I didn't "produce" I could lose my job. But what if producing for a boss or shareholders conflicts with my client's interests? As an independent advisor, I do not have a boss on Wall Street dictating to me how many clients I should acquire or what products I should sell.

The pressure that captive advisors who work for retail brokerage firms have is significant. There are two main reasons for this. The first is because the company's stock is publicly traded and, therefore, not only do advisors have clients to serve, but their bosses also have shareholder expectations to manage. The second is because retail brokerage firms have contracts with mutual fund companies that provide revenue sharing. Revenue sharing is an agreement made between a broker and a mutual fund company. If the broker sells a certain volume of the mutual fund company's products (mutual funds), the mutual fund company provides a "kickback" to the broker. In 2016, American Funds wrote a check to Edward

Jones for $59.5 million![15] Yes, Edward Jones sold so many American Funds mutual funds that they profited an extra $59 million for doing so. I used to have a friend who worked for Edward Jones. He said that the company computer-generated these three recommendations for every prospective client that he entered information for: 1) American Funds, 2) American Funds, and 3) American Funds.

If you are working with an advisor specializing in distribution strategies who is accountable by law to put your interest first (fiduciary) and does not have a boss on Wall Street (independent), you are poised to have an orderly estate. That is, of course, if he is focused on two other aspects of your estate: tax and legal. While the type of advisor we have described thus far is not a CPA or an attorney, he should be concerned with these other two disciplines.

DON'T MAKE THE IRS A BENEFICIARY

Do you like paying taxes? Do you like owing someone money? In my experience, most respond, "No." Please understand, however, that if you have tax-deferred retirement accounts, there is a tax liability on potentially one of the largest assets you own. And

---

15 "2016 Revenue Sharing Disclosure," Edward Jones, December 31, 2016 https://www.edwardjones.com/images/revenue-sharing-disclosure.pdf.

the most frightening thing about it is that the liability isn't fixed. Let me ask you, would you own a home in retirement with a variable interest rate? That sounds risky, doesn't it—the thought that if interest rates spike your payment would spike right along with it? How does this relate to your tax-deferred retirement account? When you withdraw that money (that's not "if" but rather "when"—if you wait long enough, the IRS will *require* you to withdraw that qualified money), you must pay taxes on that money. Do you know what your tax rate will be one, five, ten years from now? Is that within your control? Perhaps you want to withdraw as little as possible and leave it to your children. Do you know what taxes they will have to pay on those funds five, ten, twenty years from now? Remember, if your children receive your tax-deferred account as an inherited or beneficial IRA, the claim the IRS has on your money does not go away. When they withdraw that money, they must pay income taxes based on their individual tax rate. And if you are wondering whether your heirs will pay higher taxes than you, just look at the fiscal path our country is currently on.

It doesn't take a financial analyst or CPA to look at our country's balance sheet and tell we are heading in the wrong direction. The current Unites States debt exceeds $19 trillion. On January 11, 2011, a man by the name of David Walker appeared on national radio and made a scary prognostication. He said that, based on the current path the US is on fiscally and the debt we currently have, future tax rates will have to double or our country could go bankrupt.[16] Now, we have all heard the "gloom and doom" forecasts on television and websites, but this is one opinion that we should take seriously. Why? Who is David Walker? From 1998 to 2009, Walker was the Comptroller General for the United States and head of the Government Accountability Office. In short, he was the CPA of the US and the nation's chief auditor. He is not a news channel celebrity or a doomsday publisher trying to sell books. If he is worried, you should be too. The good news is there are steps you can take to preserve your money and protect it from the government.

THE THREE TAX BUCKETS

Your money can be grouped into three categories or "buckets" to determine how your financial landscape looks tax-wise. The first bucket is the **Taxable Bucket**. This is the money you have probably already paid taxes on, and if you invest it, you must pay taxes when you realize a return. These are non-IRA assets such as brokerage accounts, savings accounts, or

16 David McKnight, *The Power of Zero*, (Boston: Acanthus Publishing, 2013).

Certificate of Deposits at your bank. If you realize a gain in this bucket, you must pay the piper come April 15th the following year. The second bucket is the **Tax-Deferred Bucket.** These are assets such as IRAs, 401(k)s, deferred annuities, etc. These accounts generally grow tax-deferred, which means you only pay taxes when you withdraw the money. Unlike the taxable bucket, you can buy and sell holdings inside your Tax-Deferred Bucket and you don't pay taxes on the gains until you *withdraw the money.* The third bucket is the **Tax-Free Bucket**. This money grows tax free, and whether you withdraw your gains or leave it to your beneficiaries at your death, *it is tax-free,* subject to limitations. These assets include Roth IRAs and life insurance. I don't include municipal bonds in this bucket for a few reasons. The first is because to meet the requirement for the Tax-Free Bucket, the asset must be free from federal tax, capital gains tax, *and* state tax. For example, if you live in North Carolina and purchase a municipal bond in Georgia, you aren't purchasing in the municipality in which you live, so you would have to pay state taxes. Additionally, if you purchase a mutual fund of municipal bonds and your mutual fund increases and you decide to sell, you would pay capital gains tax.

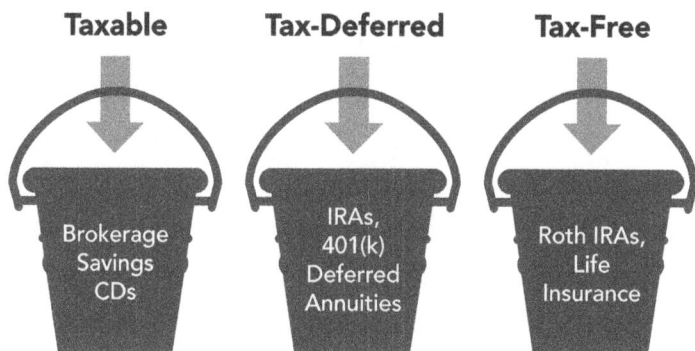

Taxable	Tax-Deferred	Tax-Free
Brokerage Savings CDs	IRAs, 401(k) Deferred Annuities	Roth IRAs, Life Insurance

As you review your portfolio, you will probably notice that you have money in each of these three tax buckets. Now, let me ask you, which bucket would you like to have most of your money in? While we might like to have most of our money in the Tax-Free Bucket, it is more common to have most of your money in the Tax-Deferred and Taxable buckets. And remember, if you owe taxes, not only is the IRS a beneficiary, but they can also change the percentage coming to them! If you are convinced you want Uncle Sam to take the smallest bite possible out of your money, there are a several strategies you can implement that will help you convert your tax-infested money into tax-free money. These strategies should be designed by professionals (both financial and tax) who specialize in this aspect of financial planning and can explain to you all of the benefits, limitations, and charges associated with any of the products you may choose for your portfolio. An orderly estate is tax-efficient.

DRAFT AN ESTATE PLAN

When I first entered financial services, one of my mentors strongly encouraged me to learn as much as possible about estate planning. He used to always say, "Anyone who owns something and loves someone needs an estate plan." If you think about that saying, the logical conclusion is that *everyone* needs an estate plan. For the purposes of this book, when I say estate plan I am referring to four main legal documents. Those documents are as follows:

- Durable General Power of Attorney
- Living Will/Health Care Surrogate
- Last Will & Testament
- Revocable Living Trust (if needed)

These documents (specifically, a last will and testament and/or trust) help your attorney, executor, successor trustee, and/or the court transfer your wealth to your heirs as you desired—*as you willed*. (I will explain more about the roles and powers you can grant to your heirs in Step Four). According to a survey conducted by US Legal Wills, 63 percent of respondents had no will at all, and only half of those over age sixty-five had a will that was up to date.[17] If

17 Tim Hewson, "Are there even fewer Americans without wills?" U.S. Legal Wills, Accessed Aug. 9, 2017, https://www.uslegalwills.com/blog/americans-without-wills/.

you die without a will, you cede control of your assets to the state in which you lived. The state's laws will determine who your heirs will be, and the state will also choose the executor of your estate. Think about that for a moment. Do you want the state deciding who your heirs are and who will manage your affairs after your death? Most would say that this is the one entity that they absolutely do not want meddling in their business and making decisions on their behalf. Why then do so many people die without a will? A recent survey of 2,000 Americans found the three main reasons so many people die without a will are: 1) procrastination, 2) belief they don't need one, and 3) cost.[18] I am not an attorney, and I want you to read the rest of this book, so I won't go into a lot of detail about drafting estate documents. There are however, a couple of mistakes that we often see in our practice which are important to review.

I NEED TO GET THAT DONE, I JUST HAVEN'T GOTTEN AROUND TO IT...

One of my favorite comedians is Brian Regan, and he has a skit about going to the eye doctor that I think about every time one of our clients is procrastinating about getting their legal documents done:

18 "Make-a-Will Survey," Rocketlawer.com.

"I'm wearing new contacts. I've just had my prescription changed after six years. Did you ever wait that long? When you get new lenses, you're like, man, I could have been seeing things! How can instantly-improved vision not be at the top of your to do list? 'Oh, I'll see tomorrow. I don't have time. I don't have time...to see clearly. No, I don't, I don't, no I can't do that. Do you see what's on my desk?'"

Everyone is busy—most of us are too busy—but if you are fifty-five years old or older, getting your estate documents drafted should be at the top of your to-do list. If you are like most human beings, there are things you procrastinate about. The thing about pro-crastination is that typically the law of consequences eventually pushes us to action. We delay taking care of this or that until the effects of our procrastination become an issue. For example, not doing laundry, not stopping for gas, or not going to the eye doctor. Not having clean clothes, running out of gas on the highway, or no longer being able to read will push you to action. The negative consequence is annoying or unavoidable, and it forces you into action. This method doesn't work in estate planning.

When it comes to drafting estate documents, once the negative consequence of your procrastination is experienced, it is too late. You can't do anything about it. If you have a stroke and your son needs to pay your electric bill and you don't have a durable general power of attorney, it is too late. If you are incapacitated and your daughter needs to make end of life decisions about your care but you don't have a living will expressing your medical treatment desires, it is too late. If you want a portion of your estate to go to charity but you don't have a will or trust detailing that desire and you pass away without one, it's too late. I am convinced that most people put off drafting an estate plan because there is no "warning sign," no consequence of procrastination until it's too late.

In their book 5 @ 55, Attorneys Judith Grimaldi and Joanne Seminara suggest that all people complete their estate documents by—yes, you guessed it— age fifty-five. They posit that by age fifty-five you have reached an age that, while the thought of death and dementia aren't the most delightful of topics to ponder, the end of life still seems far off.[19] Whether you are forty-five, fifty-five, sixty-five, or seventy-five—if you own something and you love someone, you need an estate plan. Don't put it off, and finally, don't buy documents online.

---

19 Judith D. Grimaldi and Joanne Seminara, 5@55, (Fresno: Quill Driver Books, 2015).

ONLINE LEGAL SERVICES

Over the last ten years, revenue from online legal companies have nearly doubled.[20] However, before you jump online and throw a living will in your virtual checkout basket, I encourage you to reconsider. I recently asked our partner attorney, Robert Livingston, about going online to purchase estate documents, and he made a few interesting points. He said:

"I can attest that most documents I see are drafted incorrectly. They rely on the customer to make elections without a thorough explanation of what they are choosing. Most of the time, the final document does not reflect what the customer wanted, and they don't even know it. The opportunity to establish a relationship with an actual person so they can ask questions cannot be replaced by a canned, fill-in-the-blanks program."

What Rob is saying here is that without the live interaction between a client and an attorney, the client really doesn't know whether their legal documents are consistent with their desires. What if you do go online for your legal documents—how can you find out if your online documents were drafted correctly? There are only two ways to find out. Either you pay

---

20 "Online Legal Services Market Research Report," IBISWorld.com, NAICS OD5638, January, 2017.

an attorney to review them, or you take your chances when they are used. I found it troubling (but not surprising) that Rob said *most* of the online documents he sees are drafted incorrectly. Is it worth taking that kind of chance? And what happens if a legal document you bought online gets rejected in court?

Online shoppers will have little recourse if they end up with a problematic document from an online legal company. In its terms of use, LegalZoom "makes no warranty" that the site or materials "will meet your requirements" or that the results will "be accurate or reliable."[21] RocketLawyer says in its terms of service that its information, software, products, and services "may include inaccuracies" and that "information and opinions received via the website should not be relied upon for personal, medical, legal, or financial decisions."[22]

The above information begs the question: If these online companies will not stand behind their legal documents in the fine print, should you? If you are traveling and need to purchase plane tickets, shop online. If you would like a good book to for the trip,

---

21 "Terms of Use," LegalZoom.com, last modified December 15, 2017, https://www.legalzoom.com/legal/general-terms/terms-of-use.

22 "Terms of Service," RocketLawyer.com, last modified January 5, 2018, https://www.rocketlawyer.com/terms-of-service.rl.

shop online. If you decide to get your estate documents done before you leave for the trip, go see an attorney.

WORK WITH A SPECIALIST

It is amazing how after a ten-minute internet search you can proclaim yourself an expert on any topic. Unfortunately, the internet has given us access to a breadth of information, but it lacks a few important characteristics: 1) the learning was not absorbed over time and subsequently not retained because it can be searched again, and 2) it lacks an encountering of reality that provides the depth of learning needed to really become an expert. In short, the internet provides a lot of data and information, but not wisdom.

In some ways, the concept of breadth versus depth is nothing new. There are some topics or disciplines that I know well (with depth) due to repetition and acute focus. Then there are other areas that I am familiar with and can comment on (breadth), but I am no expert. For example, I can sew a button on a dress shirt, but I cannot make my girls' Easter dresses like my wife can. I can put Neosporin on a wound, but I can't stich up a laceration. I am sure there are areas in your life, as well, that you have a *general* knowledge and other areas where you have more of a *specialized* knowledge. This is most clearly seen in the medical field—there are general practitioners, and there are specialists.

When I was young, my grandma was always going to the podiatrist. I remember thinking to myself back then, *What is a podiatrist?* Later, I learned that a podiatrist is a specialist who treats conditions of the feet. I didn't know what a podiatrist was because, as a seven-year-old boy, I never had to go to the podiatrist. As you get older, things change. Your diet changes, how well you sleep changes, how well you remember things changes, the type of doctors you see changes. The same should be true for your financial life.

When you near retirement, you need a different type of financial professional helping you plan for the future. Hopefully, the above distinctions will help you find a financial professional that is uniquely suited to help you design an orderly estate.

Step Four

ENLIGHTEN HEIRS
AND FIDUCIARIES

———

*"Only put off until tomorrow what you
are willing to die having left undone."*
—PABLO PICASSO

Memorializing your family story, strengthening family
bonds, and designing an orderly estate all set the
groundwork for this step. If you take those steps seriously, this one can be a great experience. As I have
mentioned previously, passing on more than your
money is a *project*. It is a process that will not happen
without a fair amount of time and intentionality. Since
nearly half of Americans are dying intestate (without
a will), most retirees are not devoting time to this
project, and it is safe to say most are not disclosing
their plan and desires to their heirs and fiduciaries.

For centuries, the law of succession—or inheritance law—has governed how property changes ownership when the owner dies, especially if he dies intestate. The law and customs surrounding this experience are extremely broad, and they have changed over time. Some family norms, however, such as keeping your heirs in the dark when it comes to your estate plan, haven't changed.

When the American colonies began to form and land was abundant, inheritance law began to drastically change from the traditions of England. Primogeniture—the right of succession belonging to the firstborn—was replaced with *partible inheritance*. This meant if you died without a will your assets were passed to your children in equal shares. Additionally, over the last few centuries, the spouse (specifically, the wife) has gained substantial position and protection in the law, something that had been severely lacking. However, while much of the law has changed since America was founded, there are still informal traditions surrounding the wealth transfer process that remain. A precedent surrounding the actual practice of passing on the ownership of your property, which hasn't changed much over the last few centuries, is the confidentiality of the estate plan. Regardless of the reason, retirees typically do not share much with their heirs about how their estate is structured and who will play what role (who will serve as fiduciaries). It is still common for an estate plan—and even who the heirs are—to be kept a secret.

In George Elliot's classic novel *Middlemarch,* there are a few examples of the drama that often surrounded passing on an estate in the early 1800s, which was an outcome of the "confidential" estate plan. One of the characters, Mr. Featherstone, is a wealthy aristocrat and has no children. When he becomes gravely ill, distant family members come to his home attempting to be recognized—and remembered—by Mr. Featherstone. Mr. Featherstone has a nephew, Fred, who has been in and out of good graces. He bequeathed Fred a considerable fortune but later rescinded this will due to Fred's irresponsible behavior. On his deathbed, he realizes he has two wills (one including Fred and one not) and he asks his servant, Mary, to destroy the second will. Mary refuses and begs Mr. Featherstone to wait until the morning, when a new and valid will can be drawn up. Unfortunately, Mr. Featherstone dies before this can be done. Fred and the rest of the extended family who were vying for a share of the grand estate are shocked when they learn that his estate is left to his illegitimate child that no one knew about.

This is an extreme—and somewhat humorous—

example of not disclosing the details of your estate. However, in reality it is typically much more sobering. Failing to share your estate plan with your heirs and fiduciaries is a recipe for conflict and confusion after your passing. If you have ever been involved in the settling of an estate, you may have experienced what I am describing. I am not suggesting you need to tell your children the exact dollar amounts in each of your accounts. I am suggesting that you share with your children the roles you have given (successor trustee, executor, etc.), the instruments in place (trust, will, etc.), and your intentions behind both. Transparency will help limit conflict, confusion, and surface issues that need to be addressed before your passing. More importantly, it will provide preparation for a life-changing transition for those you pass the mantel to.

A RITE OF PASSAGE

As I have worked with retirees who have taken this seriously, I have noticed that they see their children's inheritance as a *process* more than a dollar amount. Death triggers an inheritance, but there is more than just a wealth transfer that takes place. When you pass, the character and roles of your individual family members change. Today, you are the patriarch or matriarch, the elder of your family. In some ways, you represent the connection to generations of deceased ancestors. This mantle of leadership passes to your children when you die. And as we have discussed in this book, the goal is to pass on who you are along with what you have. This process of inheritance is a sort of *rite of passage*.

In his book, *Rites of Passage*, my friend Jason Craig explains that all rites of passage have three main parts: 1) separation (from one state), 2) initiation (a marked transition), and 3) incorporation (joining the new "corpus" or body with which you are now associated). For example, when you get married, you separate from your old state in life (the single life), there is an initiation (typically a wedding ceremony), and then you are incorporated into your new state of life (the "body" of a married couple) as you begin to live as newlyweds. Now, let's apply this to the rite of passage your children will go through when you pass away. Your death will separate them from you and their current state in life as an heir, their initiation will take place when they formerly receive your estate, and once complete, they will be incorporated into the body of matriarchs and patriarchs that have gone before them. They are now the elders, the link to your family patrimony. Something that important begs for preparation.

As with most rites of passage, your children will experience pain, confusion, and many challenges during this process of separation, initiation, and incorporation. They have probably experienced other rites of passage in life. For example, when your daughter passes into the new state of motherhood (with all the pain and challenges that come with it), you are there to help, guide, and love her through the process—you are present. When you die, however, *your children will go through this rite of passage without you.* You will not be there to explain why you left your watch to your youngest son or that you hope they don't sell the family farm. An inheritance is a rite of passage, and if you share your estate plan with your heirs prior to your death, it will provide a *narrative* to the decisions you made. If your children know the *why* behind your decisions, it will make the process of inheritance more meaningful.

KNOWING MORE

Recently, my wife and I bought a home on seven acres in the foothills of Western North Carolina. There are several parts of the property that are exciting for our children. When they aren't studying or doing chores, they like to get lost in the woods, play in the creek, or hike the hill behind our house. There are also interesting horticultural aspects of the property. I was told that one of the first owners was a retired landscape engineer who managed government properties in Washington, DC. Whether it is the stunning Japanese maple in front of the house or the cypress trees that line the creek bank, it's clear these early caretakers knew what they were doing.

During our first spring on the property, my son and I were trimming trees in the field to make it easier for me to mow. I had planned to tackle the project in the winter, when the trees were dormant, but the season had slipped past and spring was already upon us. I walked the path I typically take when I mow, chainsaw in hand, and Monroe followed behind me driving the tractor and trailer. As I cut down branches, he jumped off and threw them into the trailer. A short time into the project, he started yelling for me. I was on to the next tree about forty yards away and couldn't make out what he was saying. I turned off the chainsaw and started to walk back to him. He was standing at the base of the tree I had just trimmed yelling, "Apples, apples! Dad! This tree is growing apples!" Much to my surprise, small apples about the size of golf balls were scattered about the limbs of the tree. I had no idea we had an apple tree. Had I known, I wouldn't have cut nearly the number (or size) of limbs just to improve clearance for my mower.

How I wish I could sit down with all the past owners

of our property and listen to the stories lying beneath every tree. I wish I could learn the why behind all the decisions made. I am constantly trying to figure out how the electrical is run, what drainage pipe runs where, and a multitude of other unknowns. It would be a real gift to have received that knowledge before or when we bought this home. If the wisdom of this estate had been passed on, I'd have more apples and my vegetable garden wouldn't flood when it rained.

The same is true with your estate. An heir is a beneficiary. The word *beneficiary* comes from the Latin *beneficium*, meaning *bene* "well" or "good" and *ficium* which means "making." When a person is a beneficiary, there is *good done to them*. Similar words such as *benediction* have the same origin; when you receive a benediction, you receive a blessing—good is done to you. Being a beneficiary is supposed to be a *good* thing. Money aside, most executors, successor trustees, and beneficiaries will tell you their experience of receiving an inheritance was not exactly an experience of blessing. But it can be.

It may be comfortable and less confrontational to keep your estate a secret until your death, but avoiding one challenge only passes a harder one on to your children. If you approach inheritance as a rite of passage for your children, they will be better for it. If they know their future roles and the why behind your decisions, you have a better shot of *doing good to them* at your passing.

CHOOSING FIDUCIARIES

Before you share your estate plan with your heirs, you must first choose fiduciaries. I am not an attorney, and you should consult your attorney with specific questions regarding your legal affairs. But this is so important that it's a part of the five-part *Sound Retirement Blueprint* process that my brother and I are constantly educating our clients on—the importance of having legal documents completed and up-to-date. We also regularly assist in the estate-settlement process and have experienced first-hand the chaos that ensues when these tools are not in place. Choosing the right fiduciary begins with a little education, understanding the necessary roles and what that role will entail. I have found that when retirees clearly understand the roles that must be filled, they are more comfortable with their choices and more proactive with sharing their plan with their heirs and chosen fiduciaries.

DURABLE POWER OF ATTORNEY

The first fiduciary you will need to appoint is an

"attorney-in-fact" or agent under a power of attorney (POA). A power of attorney grants an agent the authority to be your legal representative for business matters. This agent could have the ability to do such things as pay bills, sell property, file taxes, etc. The power you give your POA is up to you; it can be as broad or as limited as you want.

There are both durable and non-durable powers of attorney. When you consult with your attorney to draft estate documents, he will most often recommend a *durable* power of attorney, or power of attorney with durable provisions. The word durable means that the power you have granted *endures* or *remains durable* in the event of your incapacitation. An important thing to remember is that this power is not *conditioned on your incapacitation.* This means that the day you sign the POA, your agent has full authority to act on your behalf. Therefore, when selecting an agent under a power of attorney, you will want to choose someone who is extremely trustworthy and has exercised prudence in *their own* personal decision making.

A common "short-cut" that some people will take to avoid signing a POA is simply to add their child or children as joint owners on their bank accounts. This may provide a quick remedy to some of the circumstances you might encounter (such as enabling them to immediately write checks to pay bills), but it comes with its own set of risks. For example, let's say you add your daughter to your bank account and then a few weeks later she is in a car accident. She comes out of the incident without injury, but the other driver was injured and your daughter was as fault. The other driver brings a lawsuit against your daughter. She doesn't have much in terms of assets, but since her name is on your bank account, the court sees your money as her money too. By making her a joint owner, you have unintentionally subjected your assets to her risks. While avoiding this vulnerability is one reason to have a POA, the more important reason is to have someone who can handle your business affairs if you are unable. It can be scary to grant the authority that comes with a power of attorney, but it can be an extremely useful tool in situations that are almost always unpredictable.

HEALTH CARE SURROGATE

Similar to the agent under a durable power of attorney, the health care surrogate has a role to play while you are still living. This person will be authorized to make health care decisions if you are unable to make those decisions due to incapacitation. This includes routine medical decisions such as ordering medical records or discussing your condition with a physician. It also includes end-of-life decisions based on your wishes described in your living will or health care advanced directive. While there are many reasons why it is prudent to have a living will and a health care surrogate, it is extremely important that:

- You have at least one alternate listed if your primary surrogate is unavailable, unable or unwilling.
- Current phone numbers for your surrogate and alternate(s) are listed on the document.
- Your health care directive was drafted in the state in which you live. (If you split your time between two residences [for example, Ohio and Florida], it may be wise to have a health care directive for each of the states in which you live, but you should exercise caution to ensure they are consistent.)
- You provide a copy of your health care directive/ living will to your surrogate and alternate(s). (This is mandated by statute in the state of Florida.)
- You ensure that it is current and grants authority to access medical information under HIPAA, a federal law designed to protect patient privacy.

Attorneys will often cite the well-known Terri Schiavo case when stressing the importance of having a health care surrogate. Terri did not have an advanced directive (living will) or health care surrogate designated when she fell ill. After nineteen court hearings and a battle that reached the Supreme Court, the courts sided with Michael Schiavo, and her feeding tube was removed. The lesson to learn from this tragic case is that you do not want a court making these decisions for you. While this case makes us think of end-of-life decisions, a health care surrogate can also be called upon when it *is not* an end-of-life scenario. For example, perhaps you have had a procedure and the doctors have decided to keep you heavily sedated as a safety precaution for your healing. This would be a situation where decisions might need to be made on your behalf. When choosing a health care surrogate, I tell my clients to choose someone *personally* and *geographically* close to them if possible.

One other important distinction that is commonly misunderstood is the difference between a living will and a do-not-resuscitate order (DNRO). A living will is a legal document that provides advanced guidance to your family and medical community whether or not you want artificial life support if you become ill in the future. However, it normally assumes this is the *last decision* that would need to be made after the medical community has done everything within its power to heal you and save your life. Now, let's contrast that to a do-not-resuscitate order. A DNRO tells the medical community: *Do not even try to heal me or save my life*. Do not administer CPR or take any other lifesaving actions should I be incapacitated. This is actually a medical order that is signed by a doctor and set forth on a specific form established by the state in which you live. Every state has its own version. A DNRO is generally appropriate when someone is already severely ill and is ready to pass and does not want to delay the process of dying any longer. Therefore, a living will expressing that you do not want artificial life support if you suffer from an irreversible terminal condition, and if all treatment options have been exhausted, is *very different* than a do-not-resuscitate order and should be approached with thoughtful consideration.

EXECUTOR/PERSONAL REPRESENTATIVE

Your last will and testament will appoint an executor or personal representative. The role of an executor is primarily to secure estate assets and to settle just debts and final taxes for your estate. He will submit your last will and testament to be probated by the appropriate court if necessary. The executor has the tasks of gathering up and organizing your assets with the help of your attorney and/or financial advisor. This is often called "marshalling" your assets. In Step Three: *Design an Orderly Estate*, I explained the importance of working with a retirement specialist. If you are working with an advisor who specializes in serving retirees, he will be very helpful to your executor. Marshalling your assets can be a very time-consuming and expensive project—especially if your attorney and his staff are doing most of the work. However, the right financial advisor will have what we call a *master estate summary* on file. A master estate summary lists all the assets you own—whether or not the advisor is managing the asset. For example, we have a document like this on file for every client. It contains every asset they own, who the custodian is, the tax type, who the beneficiary is, and of course the current value. It includes securities, real estate, business equity, life insurance, etc. When a client passes away, we simply print off this master estate summary and walk though it with the executor of our deceased client. We find that it saves our clients' families significant time and money. It is also an honor—and very humbling—to be asked to help a family during a sorrowful and sensitive time.

TRUSTEE

The final fiduciary you may need to designate is a successor trustee, if you elect to secure a revocable living trust. A trust is a legal declaration that essentially removes your assets from your personal ownership. If a trust is created for you, you will re-title your assets into your trust, and it becomes the "owner" of those assets. There are several reasons why an attorney may recommend this tool, such as avoiding the cost and time delays of probate, keeping your wealth transfer private (probate is a public process), or providing the opportunity to have post-mortem control of your estate. While your trust will technically own your assets, the good news is you are still in charge. You will be the first trustee of your trust. Once you pass, a successor trustee will step into the primary role as trustee. Most couples will either be co-trustees of a combined family trust, or if there are separate trusts, will reciprocally name each other successor trustee. If you are not married, you will need to name at least one successor trustee.

The role of the trustee is to manage and distribute the property held under the terms of the trust. The trustee will carry out all responsibilities designated by the trust, such as choosing investments, paying expenses, providing for your care upon incapacity, and making final distribution of assets according to your expressed wishes. The trustee may also be a beneficiary of the trust. For example, let's say you have four children but you are worried that, if they receive your assets in a lump sum at your passing, it may do more harm than good. If you have a trust, you can decide how and when the assets are distributed. And while there are four beneficiaries, you can appoint the most responsible one as the successor trustee. The guidelines I recommend when selecting a successor trustee are like those of a power of attorney; you want to choose someone who is trustworthy and has exercised prudence in their personal decision making.

One of the most common mistakes is not funding the trust. Once your attorney has drafted the trust documents, you must go through the process of re-titling your assets into your trust. Your attorney and financial advisor can help you with the process. But it is important to know that until you take this step, your trust will not provide the benefits that you had hoped for.

GET FACE-TO-FACE

Knowing the various roles that others may play for you in the future will help you make these necessary choices. After you have consulted with your attorney and drafted your estate plan, it is now time to share your plan with your heirs and fiduciaries. As I mentioned at the beginning of this chapter, sharing your estate plan will provide a form of initiation—the first rite of passage—that they will experience *without you.* My parents and several relatives have named me as a fiduciary in their estate plan. How do I know? They asked me if I would be willing and then sent me a copy of their legal documents after they were executed (the documents, that is). It is a good idea to make sure your heirs and fiduciaries have a copy of your estate plan, but it is far better to have a meeting.

One of the programs we offer our clients is our *Inheritance Design Retreat.* This is day and a half retreat during which I meet with our client and their heirs. The retreat is split into two main parts. During the first part, Generation 1 (my client) shares their Family Charter with their heirs. I will explain this process in detail in the next chapter. The second part of the retreat is walking through their estate plan and making sure that each of the heirs understand who will play what role once Generation 1 has passed. I answer questions, and my clients share, in detail, their desires for how they want their estate handled when they pass. Yes, their specific instructions are in the documents, but it is much more real hearing the *why* face-to-face.

Once, I facilitated one of these retreats for one of my clients and their four children. When we got to the living will and health care surrogate, the children learned that their father had elected not to receive artificial life support should the conditions of the living will be met. After I finished explaining my client's desires, it was very quiet in the room. I asked if anyone had any questions, and my client's daughter, who happen to be the chosen health care surrogate, spoke up. She said, "Dad, I understand what this document says, and I respect your wishes, but if you don't mind, I would like you to share verbally to all of us that this is your clear desire." Her father shared his feelings and the reason he made the decision. You could feel the tension in the room ease. With her siblings present, she could hear her father's wishes, and I could tell it took a bit of the weight off her shoulders.

The next time I will sit in a room with those four children will be after one or both of their parents have passed. And at that time, we can all lean on the shared memory of that retreat. There will be no surprises, and conflict will be minimized because we were all there. We all witnessed the matriarch and patriarch of the family share their vision (Family Charter) and their final wishes detailed in their estate plan. We had the hard conversation about death and dying. We didn't discuss the values of accounts. But we did sit there, eyeball-to-eyeball, face-to-face, and hear the heart of one generation shared with another.

If one of the heirs attempts to deviate from the vision and plan that their parents shared, the others will quickly correct. The natural accountability that a shared experience like this provides is powerful. I am confident that this family will not experience conflict and division when we meet again. It will be a rite of passage they were prepared for.

While it is helpful to have a knowledgeable third-party present when an estate plan is shared—to answer questions and provide clarification if needed—it isn't necessary. If you have an estate plan, I encourage you to gather your heirs together and share the why behind your decisions. Then, when you pass away and they transition from *heir* to *matriarch or patriarch*, your memory will comfort and guide them through the experience. Your estate plan shouldn't be a secret like it was for Mr. Featherstone's relatives. Transparency will help limit conflict, confusion, and surface issues that need to be addressed, and help prepare your family for their forthcoming inheritance.

Step Five

CREATE A FAMILY CHARTER

———

"The legacy of heroes is the memory of a great
name and the inheritance of a great example."
—BENJAMIN DISRAELI

A few years after getting married, I had lunch with
a man—we will call him John—who said something
that later changed my life. He was a very successful
executive who was married with several children,
and most would agree he "had it all together." I was a
young father with two small children, so I was asking
him for pointers on just about every topic, from disciplining your children to choosing the best family
neighborhood. At one point in the conversation, he
surprised me when he said, "Justin, you have some
good questions about family life, but I have to tell you

something. As you know, my company is headquartered in downtown Jacksonville, and I live in Ponte Vedra Beach." "Yes," I said, and he continued. "You see the thing is, when I am at work, I have a vision. I know what needs to be done, I can solve almost any problem, people respect me, and I am successful. For some reason, however, something happens to me when I drive over the intercostal waterway. When I get home, I feel like I am drifting through life rather than living with a clear vision for my family." I was extremely surprised, by both his statement and his humility.

Six years later, Angela and I were having similar feelings to what John shared with me that day. We were living in a rental, trying to pay off debt, and I knew my current job needed to change. We had always been on the same page with family decisions, but at this moment, we just weren't sure *which page we were on*. We were confused and didn't know what to do. Everything about the near future seemed uncertain. Was I going to find another job? Were we going to rent for another year? Should we be open to relocating? Where did we want to live? The questions kept coming, and we tried our best to keep up. Unfortunately, our "pros & cons" lists made us more confused.

The problem was that we were analyzing each decision in a vacuum and not taking the bigger picture into consideration. We didn't have a family vision to serve as a guide for our discernment. We were weighing the means but didn't know the end. We needed a "rule" to provide a litmus test to each option that presented itself. What I mean by that is, we needed something to point to and ask ourselves, "If we make this decision, does it honor our family vision?" or, "Will this decision bring us one step closer to realizing our family vision or distract us from it?" We were just like John; we didn't have a vision for our family.

Finally, one Saturday afternoon, Ang and I were sitting in our living room discussing the future. Instead of jumping into the most urgent decision of the day, I asked her how she would describe our family vision. We discussed faith, family, and finances, but we were having trouble pinpointing exactly what that vision was. Finally, a question came to mind "What do we want our grown children to be like?" It seemed like a simple question, but it forced us to engage our imagination and picture our family far into the future. That day, we ended up spending four hours drafting the principles and character traits of our grown children. After that, we broke down each character trait and asked ourselves what would need to be present in their lives today in order to develop each character trait.

For example, part of our vision states, "We want our children to be skilled in the home and on the land." We want our girls to know how to sew a dress or bake bread from scratch, and we want our boys to know how to swing a hammer or care for livestock. This sort of detail helped us tremendously and ended up being our guide for discernment. When the perfect house *in a gated community* came into view, it was an easy decision—you can't care for livestock in a gated community. When a decision came up, we just measured it against our family vision. If it agreed with the vision, we were a go; if it didn't agree with the vision, we decided against it. Thanks to the family vision we sketched out that Saturday afternoon, we are now living our family vision. It wasn't an easy path, and many of our decisions along the way may not have made sense from the vantage point of a bystander. At the end of the day, however, we knew our decisions were being tested against our vision, and the result has been beautiful.

It is easy to drift though life without a vision. Our culture today tends towards production and consumption. Produce something better, faster, or cheaper, and focus on your wants until you believe they are needs. It is not widely taught to be at rest, to engage your imagination, and to gaze into the future (none of these contribute to the GDP or Uncle Sam).

It is a constant battle to turn off the screens and live intentionally. I think most families have a general vision for their family, but it hasn't been spoken and, in most cases, it hasn't been detailed out in writing. The fact is, you can have good intentions and desires for your family and still drift like my friend John admitted he was doing. The simple act of writing something down makes it more real.

Perhaps you might be thinking at this point, "I am retired; it is too late to cast a vision for my family. My children are grown. I missed the boat." Or maybe you feel as though you did live according to a family vision, albeit not one typed out and hanging on the wall in your living room. Regardless of where your family has been and where they are now, the thing about a family vision is that it is *dynamic and it survives you.* Whether you feel your children are living contrary to your standards or right in line with them, there are good reasons for you to cast a vision for your clan. So, I ask you, what experiences are necessary for your grandkids to be able to catch a vision in keeping with your family? How do you hope they live their life? Creating what I call a *Family Charter* will help you define your vision, which can serve as a life compass for generations.

INTERGENERATIONAL FOCUS

A clear vision helps your family imagine and pursue a certain ideal. It serves as a sort of guardrail for decision making so that an ideal can be realized. When I facilitate an *Inheritance Design Retreat,* I have the client's family create a *Family Charter.* The main reason I use the word *charter* is because a charter is traditionally something that is given. In its most common use, a charter is a document given by a governing body or organization that outlines rights and privileges. It is a commissioning, or granting of authority. If I am chartered, I have the freedom to act on behalf of or in union with the body that granted me that authority. I have been given privilege through my association with a higher power. A charter is something that is bestowed.

This is the main difference between a family *vision* and a Family *Charter.* A husband and wife can have a family vision for their future. A Family Charter, however, implies that there is a lower body—another generation—that can receive the charter as a gift. A Family Charter also implies authority. The body who charters has more authority than the body who receives the charter. In our culture, the word authority has a negative connotation. When used appropriately, however, authority is life-giving. *One of the greatest gifts of authority is the ability to give it away*. As the matriarch and patriarch of your family, you have authority. When your children were young, your authority was exercised explicitly through being a parent. When your children are grown, however, your authority does not go away. Yes, your adult children don't have to do what you say, but authority doesn't go away; it just changes. You have gained wisdom, and it's important to find fruitful ways to share it, provided you took Step Two: *Restore and Strengthen Family Bonds* seriously and opened up the channels of communication through reconciliation.

I have an old friend and mentor by the name of Jim Galbraith who is ninety-four years old. Jim was the youngest of seven, and at the age of twenty-two, he was a B-17 Aircraft Commander in WWII. Jim and his wife, Lois, are not only the patriarch and matriarch of their eight children and twenty-one grandchildren, but they are in some ways the matriarch and patriarch of their entire community in Tallahassee, Florida. Jim is suffering from Parkinson's disease, but he remains to be one of the most interesting and influential men I know. If Jim is in a room and starts to tell a story, everyone becomes silent in anticipation. The sage is about to speak, and you don't want to miss it. He speaks with authority. Not because of his power, but rather because of his position among his family and friends. His wisdom exceeds that of younger generations, and they know it.

You possess the same authority with your family that Jim has with his. Wisdom is not something that is earned with advanced degrees or expert skills using a search engine. Wisdom is developed by years of prudent decision making. It is this sort of experience, it is wisdom that gives you authority in your family. The problem is younger generations have trouble recognizing it, or past family conflict has made it more difficult to receive.

If you have abused your authority, it is possible your relationships with your heirs have suffered or been completely severed as a result. That is why Step Two: *Restore and Strengthen Family Bonds* is such an important step. If you have a vision for your family, it should be intergenerational—it should survive you and help link generations together. If your relationship with your heirs isn't as strong as you would like, even after attempting to reconcile, you're in luck. As I will explain, creating a Family Charter is fruitful for families with weak intergenerational relationships and for those with strong ones. First, however, let's review the structure of the Family Charter.

STRUCTURE OF THE FAMILY CHARTER

In Step One: *Capture Your Story*, we discussed the importance of taking time to reflect on the experiences in your own life as well as the stories of your ancestors. My experience quitting football and then being corrected by Coach Rapp instilled the principle *Biances never quit*. Learning the story about my grandpa leaving his dishonest cousin's company, despite having a wife and three children to feed, taught me that *Biances live with integrity no matter what*. These are not just morality mantras, but experiences that led to wisdom, tradition, and a worthy narrative. These life experiences and family stories have influenced the way I live. Are family stories and life experiences the only factors that have affected my formation? No, but they have provided a sort of identity and expectation. In a word, they have given me a vision for what it means to be a Biance.

The process of creating a Family Charter is designed to help you use the stories you unearthed in Step One and draw out principles from them. Once the principles are defined, the next step is to layout indicators. Indicators provide a bit more color for family members; they help members know whether or not they are living out the principles. With stories, principles, and indicators, you have a defined a usable guide for your family to follow. I like to use the analogy of a tree when drafting a Family Charter. The Stories are the Roots, the Principles the Trunk, and the Indicators are the Fruit.

Every tree has roots, and every family has a story. And just as every part of a tree is connected to the roots, so too every family member is connected to generations of stories and life experiences that have shaped the family over time. The roots of a tree are hidden, but they provide nourishment and stability to the entire tree. Your family story can provide similar nourishment and connectedness for future generations. The trunk (principles) of the tree has grown out of the roots (family story), and the tree's life bursts forth from the trunk of the tree. If you want to grow and produce fruit, you have to be connected to the trunk of the tree. The whole tree suffers if there's weakness or wounding in between the limbs and root. If a limb is severed from the trunk, it can no longer produce fruit. If a limb is producing fruit, it is a good *indication* that it is connected to the tree. "You will know them by their fruits."[23]

When I help clients draft their charter, we use this analogy to cover three main areas of life: Faith, Family, and Finances. The stories that my clients share, and the principles derived from them, typically

---

23 Mat 7:16 RSV

fall into one of these three categories. Let's illustrate a real example using someone whose "fruit" shows an aversion to debt—but there's more to it:

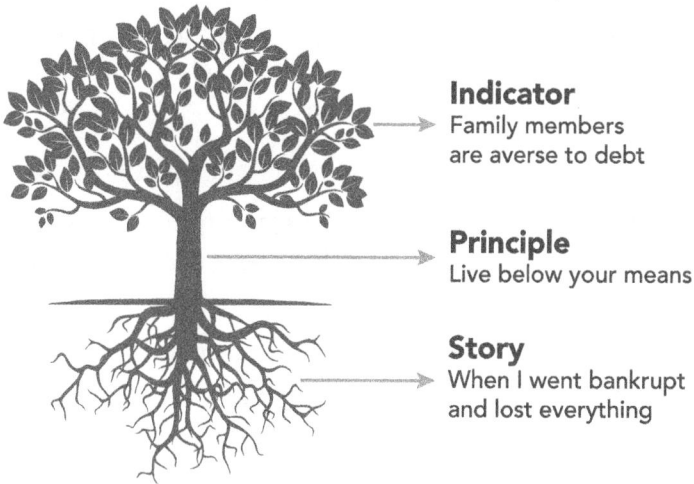

Indicator
Family members are averse to debt

Principle
Live below your means

Story
When I went bankrupt and lost everything

As you can see, beginning with the roots, we have identified a family story. That story has brought forth a principle. Finally, the way we can examine ourselves to know if we are living in accordance with that principle is by looking at the fruit. Someone averse to debt (and not in it) has likely lived below or within their means, and this likely stems from something deeper, like the story of going bankrupt.

Remember, the principles you choose *must be rooted in story*. Your story, your parents story, your grandparents story—these principles cannot be textbook theories. As I have mentioned previously, sharing a principle void the lesson learned in humility has a good chance of falling on deaf ears. If you fell on your face in life and that is why you are passionate about a certain principle, make sure you share the details of how bad the dirt tasted along with the resulting principle.

Now, living below your means is a good goal, a solid principle to live by, but how will your family members know if they are living within their means? If I am a member of a family that believes in the principle "live below your means," a good indicator might be whether or not I use debt, such as credit cards, to purchase things I can't afford. A lofty principle can often seem vague or unattainable. That is why it is helpful to have indicators.

When I think about the fruit section of the Family Charter, I often think of a little exercise common to Catholics called the *Examination of Conscience*. This exercise helps you review your words, thoughts, and actions at the end of a day. Often, a list of questions guides you to help you recall your behavior as well as the moments you experienced God's grace that day. This little guide makes it easier to pinpoint short-comings that need to be confessed and blessings that need to be recognized in gratitude. Similarly, the indicators of the Family Charter help heirs gain a pulse on how they are living. It is a tool, or list of tangible statements that helps family members indicate whether they are living the principle in question.

If one of your heirs started using a credit card and racked up $20,000 of debt, the hope is the Family Charter would be something you could review together. We will cover mentorship in the next chapter, but the Family Charter can be a powerful tool for mentorship by looking at narrative and principle before condemning, which can isolate someone that likely already realized they've made mistakes. There is a big difference between engaging your debt-ridden heir and saying, "You need to cut up those credit cards!" and saying, "Let me tell you about when I lost everything."

When completed, the Family Charter is a broad collection of stories, principles, and practical indicators that the family can enjoy for generations. It is a way to codify your family DNA, to establish a sort of creed that describes the belief-system of your family. This family tree is different from the family tree you created in grade school or the one you can build on Ancestry.com. This family tree provides more than just names; it provides the stories and principles that help your family vision come alive. The process of creating a Family Charter will help you make it more tangible for younger generations. This is important because there may not have been a time in history when generations viewed the world more differently.

TIMES HAVE CHANGED

There is a lot of research surrounding the differences between generations, especially the differences between these four: 1) the "Silent" Generation (born between 1925 and 1946), 2) the "Baby Boomer" Generation (born between 1946 and 1964), 3) Generation X (born between 1965 and 1980), and (4) the Millennial Generation (born between 1981 and 1997). If you are curious just how different the generations are, you can review the data gathered by Pew Research in February of 2010. Pew's study was quite thorough and perhaps the most comprehensive examination of the Millennial Generation ever conducted. One part of the study I found uniquely interesting was on the topic of identity. The study asked an open question, "What makes your generation unique?" [24]

---

24 "Millennials – A portrait of Generation Next," Pew Research, February, 2010, p.12.

MILLENNIAL	GEN X	BOOMER	SILENT
1. Technology use (24%)	Technology use (12%)	Work ethic (17%)	WW II, Depression (14%)
2. Music/Pop culture (11%)	Work ethic (11%)	Respectful (14%)	Smarter (13%)
3. Liberal/ tolerant (7%)	Conservative/ Trad'l (7%)	Values/ Morals (8%)	Honest (12%)
4. Smarter (6%)	Smarter (6%)	"Baby Boomers" (6%)	Work ethic (10%)
5. Clothes (5%)	Respectful (5%)	Smarter (5%)	Values/Morals (10%)

As you pan across the study above—from right to left—you might notice that the Silent Generation and the Millennial Generation only share one identification in common: being smarter (which is not exactly a unifying principle). If you are part of the Boomer or Silent Generations, you can see the obstacles you may face when sharing your Family Charter with your heirs. If you want to pass on your values—for example, regarding work ethic or morality—it may not be easily received.

It is also interesting to see the element of "story" found in the older generations. The Silent Generation identifies with their experience of WWII and the Great Depression. The Boomer Generation noted "Baby Boomers" as a top response to the question; they believe their "birth story" makes them unique. Whether it is WWII or the cohort born after the war, these life experiences, these stories, were so instrumental it became part of the character of an entire generation. Once again, your story is closely related to your value system. Without story, without the roots of the tree, it is hard to stand for outside principles. The responses of the more recent generations are less focused on story and, subsequently, less focused on principles.

There is both good and bad when it comes to analyzing any generation. The purpose of commenting on the most recent generations is not to place one generation above another. My clients do not need research results to tell them about the problems they believe are rampant in our culture. The purpose of understanding the generation of your heirs is so that you may accomplish the goal of leaving behind more than your money. Energy spent leaving a gift is one side of the coin, the other side is spending energy ensuring the gift will be received. But the greatest obstacle you may face is drawing your grown children back into the fold, back into your vision for your family. Not necessarily because of conflicting belief systems, but because to them, the very concept of *belonging* to something is foreign.

THE HEADWIND OF INDIVIDUALISM

From the Apostles Creed to the Constitution, countries, organizations, and religions—all sustainable bodies—have always passed on the stories, principles, and beliefs which bind them together. It's what "makes" them. A constitution, creed, or charter defines what it means to be a part of a body. It outlines the shared principles that members of the body accent. Your family is a small but real society, it is the "body" your Family Charter defines.

The very act of belonging to a body is counter-cultural in the world today. To belong to a body, part of your belief system must align with it. For example, if "I" don't want to go to football practice I must sacrifice what "I" want for the sake of the body—in this case, my team. And just as to be part of a body may require sacrifice, it is either that or I must sacrifice being part of the body. If I want to make every decision and only live by those things that I decide are important, then I must sever myself from the body to do so. I must sacrifice being part of the body in order to maintain my absolute individualism. As the adage goes, "there is no 'I' in team". If you are part of a body, you can't be an absolute king or god anymore. What happens if a soldier chooses himself rather than his brother soldiers (the body) in the field of battle? Not good. That is why training in the military is so rigorous; it is hard to kill your ego and live within/for a body.

Belonging to a body, and the sacrifice that this entails, is important to understand as it is possible your heirs might not like the idea of a Family Charter. During one of our Inheritance Design retreats, I was helping my clients present their Family Charter to their five children. After they were finished sharing the charter, one of the sons spoke up and said, "I understand what they say our family principles are, and *I respect that,* but I don't agree with it, nor do I plan to live that way." There were several reasons why he responded in such a way, but one of the reasons was that the Family Charter challenged his individualism. The authority from which his parents spoke was threatening. If he were to live by the principles his parents just laid out, he would have to say no to himself to say yes to the body. Was this a problem for my clients? It was expected, and it continues to be a challenge, but it was very good that the Family Charter surfaced the issue. I'm not promising this will smooth it over, but I think it is safe to challenge, or at least expose, the spirit of individuality. Coincidentally, this son was also partly living off his parents' support. After the retreat, my clients told me that they had shared with him the inconsistencies of his actions. He was enjoying the benefits of the family (body) but was unwilling to live the principles of the family. I'm guessing this little exercise is going to bring about some "adjustments."

UNFINISHED

While challenging individualism won't be easy, drafting and presenting your Family Charter to your heirs is still worth it. My clients who have issues with their heirs have found creating a Family Charter very beneficial. If handled with care, creating and presenting your Family Charter to your heirs helps you get a quantifiable gauge as to how far outside your family vision your children may be operating. You probably already know which children would struggle with the process. The good news is that after this experience you can begin to repair and strengthen these relationships. The specific tenets that your heirs object to may be telling as to where restoration may be needed. On one retreat, I had a daughter of one of my clients say, "This is difficult for me because I didn't witness my parents living these principles when I was young." After the retreat, my clients used that moment of honest sharing to engage their daughter and restore the relationship.

Angela and I have dear friends who are parents of four grown children. All four are married with great spouses and are raising children of their own. When I think about their family, I am amazed at the unity they enjoy. As the matriarch and patriarch, I know our friends have experienced both joy and sorrow in their family, but no matter what the circumstance, they still take their role as parents seriously. As their children have married, they have simply "adopted" their sons- and daughters-in-law. They respect their children's own families, but they continue to take their role as torch-bearer of the family seriously. They believe that being a parent doesn't end; it just shifts to being a life-long mentor. Your children are unfinished, as we all are, and it's in the light of the wise that we grow.

START SMALL

Creating a Family Charter will help your family live within your vision as well as provide a framework to help you mentor your heirs. One of my clients has a prayer written by his grandfather, which is still read at Easter and Thanksgiving dinner every year. When the family gathers for these celebrations, one of the past patriarchs is remembered. And as the prayer is read, each person is reminded of what it means to be a member of the family. I have other clients who had one of their children capture an interview on film. They produced a short video that included family stories and principles, which I am sure will be passed on for generations.

Is it necessary to spend hours and even days developing a Family Charter? No. But, maybe, yes. Perhaps it is simply authoring a family prayer or being intentional about discussing family principles at your next family reunion. The goal is to share your family vision. Share it in a way that makes your heirs think about their own family vision. I have clients tell me all the time that they don't know where the years went. They can relate to my friend John; they feel like life slipped by when they were younger. If you don't want your heirs to drift through life, share your family vision with them—it's not too late.

Through sharing your story and defining your family principles, you are leaving much more than money when the family torch is passed to your heirs. You are providing the roots that will keep your children's children connected to your vision long after you have left this earth.

Step Six

BUILD A CULTURE
OF MENTORSHIP

———

*"One of the greatest values of mentors is the ability
to see ahead what others cannot see and to help
them navigate a course to their destination."*
—JOHN C. MAXWELL

My first job out of college was working for the Boy
Scouts of America (BSA) in Jacksonville, Florida. The
position I took with the BSA was the Career Explor-
ing Executive for North Florida. My job was to meet
with CEOs of companies from various industries
and invite them to start a career-mentoring program
for youth in their business. It was one of the best
on-the-ground learning experiences of my life. I was
twenty-two years old, and every day of the week I
was suiting up and meeting with the top decision

makers from some of the largest, most successful companies in Northeast Florida. Several of them became personal mentors and are still dear friends of mine today. While working in the "mentoring" department of the BSA, I began to see how effective mentoring was.

As I reflected on my own experience of mentorship, I realized that I had many good (and a few not-so-good) mentors growing up. One pivotal experience was being mentored in college by a religious community[25] of brothers called the Brotherhood of Hope. These "modern day monks" ignited my faith through their mentorship. They sought me out, remembered my name, and took a personal interest in my formation. They didn't water down hard truth to get me in the door, but they shared that teaching through relationship. They also introduced me to several other priests and laymen who also played a role in my formation during college. This intense experience of mentorship was a change from growing up in a fatherless home.

As I continued to work for the BSA, I began to view

---

25 In the Catholic Church, a "religious community" is most often a group of "consecrated" men or women that live a particular spirituality in community. The more commonly understood word is "monk" or "nun," but strictly speaking, a monk lives in a monastery, and these mentors lived "in the world," working on a college campus.

the world through the lens of mentorship. If I experienced a success in my life, I could point to a past or current mentor; if I noticed a shortcoming, there was a void of mentorship in that specific area or an instance where I had actually picked up a vice or habit that was damaging.

All these thoughts circled my mind and heart until finally a dear friend and mentor encouraged me to begin journaling my reflections on the topic. In my own life, the mentorship void was really a generational issue and, more specifically, a fatherless issue. My experience of fatherlessness was not unique—43 percent of children in the United States live in a fatherless home.[26] I began to draft a vision for a faith-based mentoring program that would provide a framework for helping fathers intentionally pass on their faith to their sons.

The pieces were coming together to launch a nonprofit organization called Fraternus (Latin for "brotherly"). Churches would sponsor the program, and boys would be mentored by the men of their church. This would create a brotherhood of disciples, a sort of fraternity of brotherhood and mentorship. The need was close to my heart, and thanks to my time with the Boy Scouts of America, I had a

---

26 US Census Bureau.

reference point for how things could take shape organizationally. Launching the organization was quite an experience of mentorship for me. Ironically, my dad gave me a book entitled *The One-Page Business Plan*, which I used to draft my first plan. That plan grew and was ultimately funded. We launched the organization in 2008, and the publishing of this book occurs on our ten-year anniversary. There have been a lot of challenges and mistakes made along the way, but now there are Fraternus chapters in eight states, and we have over 1,000 members. I hope the reach of the Fraternus mission continues to grow throughout the country. One of my greatest passions is equipping one generation to mentor the next.

Most people would agree that children need good mentors, but the question I pose is this: does that need end once a child reaches the magical age of eighteen? Tell me, have you learned anything valuable about life since your eighteenth birthday? Better yet, have you learned anything valuable about life since your thirtieth birthday? I assume you would answer yes. The need for mentorship doesn't end; *it changes*. Yes, your children need you to mentor them. Perhaps they have advanced degrees and busy lives. So what? As I have mentioned in this book, you are a reservoir of wisdom through life experience (including your mistakes) that needs to be shared.

Your friends on the golf course might not benefit from your wisdom, but your children will.

If this is true, we need to lay out some practical tenets for becoming a good mentor and making sure it happens. The principles I lay out in this chapter are principles that I know work. I have been mentored by people who use them, I have mentored others using them, and they are the very bones of Fraternus and similar organizations.

DESEGREGATION

Prior to the Industrial Revolution, it was much more common for a home to house multiple generations. Typically, the trade of the father linked the generations together. The patriarch (Generation 1) was "phasing out" of his craft and was cared for by his children's family. The son (Generation 2) had learned from his father and taken over the family enterprise. The grandson (Generation 3) would be mentored into the trade when he came of age. With three generations living on one property—or under one roof—there was a natural and constant mentorship taking place. Not only was mentorship happening with the grandfather-father-son relationships, but also with the grandmother-mother-daughter relationships. The home was a small society where the wisdom of the older generations "rubbed off" on the younger generations. And while I am sure it wasn't a perfect society, there wasn't as great a need for intentionality—mentoring wasn't on anyone's to-do list; it just happened. The multigenerational family provided the most natural medium for mentorship.

Times have changed, and generations have become more segregated. With the boom of the nursing home and assisted living facilities, grandma and grandpa now live out their final years among their peers rather than with their children. I have heard my mom (and dozens of clients) say, "I don't want to be a burden on my children," more times than I can count. And while there is truth to the struggle that comes with caring for your parents, there is also great blessing. Unfortunately, the word "senior" today is only revered when it is attached to a productive mode or state in life. The titles Senior Manager or Senior Sales Executive are badges of honor in the business world. Everything changes when you attach that word to a non-productive state in life; the title Senior Citizen is a label placed on old-timers who have nothing to offer society or younger generations. Nothing could be further from the truth.

There is even segregation of generations in the church. Regardless of denomination, Sunday school in most churches is a segregation of generations, not an experience of mentorship in the faith. Youth are segregated from older generations so the message can be communicated in a more "relevant" way. It is a good thing the apostles didn't adopt this method; some of my favorite scripture passages come from Paul writing to his "beloved son" Timothy.

Whether it is in the home or at church, there is less interaction among generations. And with less intergenerational interaction, there is less natural mentorship—the timeless concept of mentorship is vanishing from popular culture. Who needs a mentor if you have YouTube? If you wish to pass on more than your money, you need a plan. Not necessarily a plan for making time for your children (although that is good), but rather a plan for how you will approach mentorship. As I have explained above, the *natural environment* for mentoring is less common, and as a result, there are fewer people who are *natural mentors*. Therefore, in the following pages I will lay out some principles that are essential to becoming an effective mentor to your children.

THE LAW OF CONSEQUENCES

If you are retired, I am most likely a similar age and generation to your heirs. Owning a business that serves "Generation 1" and being a member of "Generation 2" has given me an interesting perspective on this intergenerational dynamic. When I am sitting in a room with a retiree and their adult children, I can immediately notice when a breakdown of communication begins to take place. I hear how something is *said*, how it is *heard*, and the gap between the two. One of the more common tensions I witness between the generations is when a patriarch and/or matriarch is torn between *providing for* and *enabling* their adult children.

There has been a steady increase in the number of young adults (twenty-five to thirty-five years old) living at home with their parents. A recent study showed that, in 2018, nearly 15 percent of young adults between the ages of twenty-five and thirty-five will be living at home with their parents. That percentage has doubled since 1981.[27] There are several causes one could argue as to the reason for the rise in adult children depending on their parents, but there is one that I think is relevant to the topic of mentorship.

---

27 "Millennials are the generation most likely to live at home," Pew Research, May 5, 2017, http://www.pewresearch.org/fact-tank/2017/05/05/its-becoming-more-common-for-young-adults-to-live-at-home-and-for-longer-stretches/ft_17-05-03_livingathome_bygen2/.

In Step Four: *Enlighten Heirs and Fiduciaries*, I wrote about the rite of passage your children will experience when you pass away. That rite of passage will not be the last they will experience in life, and hopefully it won't be the first. I hope it won't be the first, because there are several moments early in life when we should experience a "severing" of an old way and an "incorporation" into a new way of life. One of the characteristics of a rite of passage—which Jason Craig notes in his enlightening book—is that it includes some sort of challenge, struggle, or ordeal.[28] Whether it is childbirth for a woman transitioning into motherhood, boot camp for a civilian transitioning into the military, or hazing that a freshman shortstop endures after being bumped up to varsity, it isn't hard to notice the reality of this phenomenon. One not-so-formal rite of passage that young adults need to experience is living on their own.

I have listened to several clients over the years struggle with allowing their heirs to experience this rite of passage. Unfortunately, when this happens, the heir does not receive the human formation necessary for their own survival. What is the result? Perpetual adolescence. The challenge, struggle, and ordeal of having to live on your own *produces something*. It

28 Jason Craig, "Rites of Passage: How Boys Grow Up and Why Some Men Don't," *(Our Sunday Visitor)* p.72.

produces an experience of reality that isn't encountered as a child. A mentor of mine once told me that the law of consequences is one of the best teachers. It corrects you when you make a mistake, and it helps you realize that you are not God. Yes, there may be pain, there may be struggle, and as a parent, it is difficult to watch your children suffer. If you are honest with yourself, however, can you think of one good thing in your life that didn't require some sort of struggle? An achievement that didn't require a little blood, sweat, and tears? If you want to mentor your children to greatness, you first must allow them to join your world. And if they are still financially dependent, it is time to usher them through this rite of passage. Then, once they have entered your world, you must treat them like the adult they have become.

YOUR WORLD

One important concept to remember before you mentor your children is that mentoring is not parenting. I know this seems like common sense, but you might be surprised how easy it is to approach your children as a parent. I have witnessed family, friends, and clients unintentionally fall into this habit, and the results are typically not very fruitful. Comments such as, "What do I know?" echo from the delivering party, and comments such as, "I can't do anything right," come from the receiving party. When your children reach adulthood, they have entered your world. You must appeal to them as fellow adults, not grown children who should know better.

My mom works for me and Jason in our practice. The year after she retired from teaching, we opened our office and she joined the team. In fact, she hosted an "open house" at our new office and personally invited every person in the county that she knew. To this day, if you happen to be nearing retirement or have retired without coming in for a meeting, be prepared for an invitation. It doesn't matter if she runs into you at a restaurant or Publix (which she frequents almost daily), she is ready to talk about "her boys." I never thought my mom would work for me, but it has been a blessing having her around, and our clients love her. One of the neat things about having mom in the office is how teachable and lead-able she is when it comes to her role. She is always ready and eager to learn a new task, and she is an absolute perfectionist. She respects my leadership, and while she is my mom, she treats me like a fellow adult. We live in the same world.

My mom and I work well together for several reasons, but one of those reasons is that she doesn't treat me like her child. Another reason it works in our situation is because it is a mother-son relationship, not a mother-daughter or father-son relationship. I have found that when a father or mother approaches their adult child as a parent, it is typically in the father-son and mother-daughter relationships. Whether it is a mother making side comments about her daughter's parenting skills or a father giving unsolicited advice to his adult son, it is more common for the "parenting" to surface with these relationships. I could go on as to why I think this is the case, but that's not the point; the reason I mention this dynamic is to alert you to it. Part of being a good mentor is recognizing—and avoiding—natural tendencies that are counterintuitive to mentoring. Fathers, your sons have entered your world; mothers, your daughters have entered your world. Approach them as fellow adults and watch their receptivity increase.

EARN THE RIGHT TO BE HEARD

Imagine coming to work and being asked to attend a meeting in the conference room. You sit down, and your boss introduces the consultant he just hired to help improve the results of your department. He is going to analyze your work and tell you how to make improvements. Sound like fun? This is when the eye-rolling begins. Now, contrast that experience to another. Imagine you are mowing your front lawn and the mower suddenly turns off. It has plenty of gas, but you are not handy with small engines, so you don't know what to do. Luckily, you look across the street, and your friend and neighbor who is a retired mechanic happens to be outside. He immediately begins to walk across the street to show you what might be wrong and what to do to fix the mower. What's the difference between the consultant and the neighbor? The neighbor has earned the right to be heard through friendship, and the consultant is a stranger with an opinion.

I came across a webpage once that had several jokes about consultants. They were quite funny. One of my favorites was, "After it's all said and done, there is a hell of a lot more said than done." The interesting thing about a consultant is that there are many similarities to a mentor. The goal of a consultant is to help a person—or group of people—by providing perspective and experience that may be lacking. A mentor has a similar task. When you compare the two, both the consultant and the mentor are trying to help someone solve a problem or improve by sharing their own insight and expertise. Why then do you think that the role of "consultant" is met with eye-rolling while the role of "mentor" is viewed in a better light? In short, it is because the consultant-consultee dynamic is often exercised *outside of friendship*. A mentor has earned the right to be heard; the consultant has not.

If stranger/consultant is at one end of a spectrum and friend/mentor is at the other end, where do you fall in relation to your adult children? In Fraternus, the mentoring organization I started, we tell our mentors that they must *earn the right to be heard* with those they hope to mentor. Don't approach them as a problem to be fixed. If advice isn't offered through relationship, it is difficult to receive. I've been in a large city and have seen preachers on a street corner shouting scripture passages, delivering "fire and brimstone" to all who walk past. As a Christian, I am troubled by this example. I suppose it takes a bit of courage to be so bold, but the reason it frustrates me is that this person is attempting to preach to people *outside of relationship.* The street-corner preacher hasn't earned the right to be heard with those who are walking by and, therefore, they pay no attention. Worse yet, they resent it. And, I would add, it's easier to yell from a corner than to enter into the heart of another person.

As a father or mother, you have earned a certain right to be heard with your adult children. The relationship you have with them, however, must still be fostered and cared for just like other relationships. You can live in the same house with your spouse, but that relationship must be nurtured. Family bonds are not kept by name and proximity alone. If your relationship with your children isn't cared for, you begin to lose the right to be heard with them. Your heart may desire to share valuable advice with them, but when you deliver it, they subconsciously reject it. It is advice that is difficult to receive from a stranger/consultant. Therefore, paying attention to your friendship with your adult children is worthwhile.

PROPOSE VS. IMPOSE

If you are treating your children like the adults they are and caring for your relationship with them, the next habit worth practicing is a little rule I like to call *propose rather than impose*. The dictionary defines imposing as something to be endured, fulfilled, or obeyed.[29] I often sit at my two-year-old daughter's bedside and wait for her to fall asleep. If I don't, she will escape. At this age, I can impose bedtime as much as I want, but she talks to herself and does somersaults in her bed until she finally falls over asleep. I want to tell her how wonderful it is to sleep. I want to tell her that she will regret this for the rest

---

29 impose, Dictionary.com, *Dictionary.com Unabridged*, Random House, Inc., accessed: January 11, 2018, http://www.dictionary.com/browse/impose.

of her life (if she could remember). She doesn't seem to understand, and frankly, she doesn't seem to care. Imposing your will on your adult children is like imposing your will on a two-year-old. They may be clueless to what you see clearly, and it may seem like your words don't carry much weight. If they would just listen to you, everything would get better. If your adult children don't heed your advice, it could be for one of the reasons I have already covered; however, it could also be the nature of your delivery.

We all know *the way* something is said can be just as important as *what* is said. This little kernel of truth didn't get the attention it deserves until a mentor pointed it out to me. He shared with me the concept of proposing a thought, comment, or suggestion rather than imposing it. I must confess, this is still a challenge, but being aware of it greatly helps. For example, let's say you have noticed that your son is having difficulty parenting your grandson. You are at their home for a visit, and as you watch your son and grandson interact, you notice that your grandson does not obey your son. You also notice that when he doesn't obey, there is no consequence. After the kids are asleep for the night, you and your son are sitting in the living room and you say, "I know you don't believe in spanking, but if you don't start disciplining that boy it will only get worse as he gets older." Your comment seems to be ignored, until your son finally responds sarcastically, "Thanks for the advice, dad." Your attempt to "help" has angered your son and not helped the situation at all. You see the problem (disobedience) and you decide to make a suggestion (discipline), but that suggestion is received as imposing by your adult son.

Now let's rewind that scenario and review an alternative method. After the kids are asleep for the night, you and your son are sitting in the living room and you say, "That little boy sure is strong willed. I bet you're tired at the end of a day..." "You better believe it, dad," replies your son. At this point, you have expressed empathy and begun to create an opportunity to continue the dialogue. "Has he responded to anything you have tried in terms of discipline?" Now you have given your son the benefit of the doubt, and rather than offering a suggestion, you have asked a question. "We have tried timeout and taking away toys, but it doesn't seem to help," your son says. You remain silent and wait for an invitation, then your son continues, "If you have any ideas, I'd love to hear them." With the invitation, you share your thoughts and ideas.

I know every interaction with your children, or any loved one for that matter, doesn't go as smoothly as

I just described, but the question is: Where on the spectrum does most of your mentoring communication fall? In case you missed it, the process of proposing instead of imposing goes like this:

- Express empathy
- Assume the best (benefit of the doubt)
- Seek to understand (ask questions)
- Wait for an invitation
- Propose a suggestion

The process of proposing is a difficult habit because it requires patience. You may know the exact disciplining method that will solve your son's problems, but what you *don't* know is how it must be shared in order that it is received and implemented. That is why the above process is so effective. While you may know the solution, your solution is worthless unless you know how it must be delivered. Not knowing how you should say something keeps you in a humble posture and gives the recipient a chance to be humble as well, by their openness to receive guidance.

THE PURSUIT

I hope the above concepts help you mentor your adult children. Don't forget that every suggestion in this step should be built upon Step Two: *Restore and Strengthen Family Bonds*. Resolving conflict with your children, no matter how small, will make this step much easier.

I was at a wedding many years ago that touched me deeply. The bride and groom had written their own vows. As I sat and listened, one of the promises the groom made caught my ear. He said, "I will never stop pursuing your heart." At the time, I had been married for a few years, and I asked myself, "Am I still pursuing Angela's heart like I did when we were courting?" I have continued to ponder that promise and applied it to many of my closest relationships. When I think about it, the relationships that are pursued are some of the strongest relationships I have. The ones that I take for granted or do not actively pursue are weaker.

When I visit with retirees, I often hear that their children live too far away and are too busy to bother. My mom and I talk regularly, but if we happen not to talk for a week, she often says she wanted to call but every time she thought of it she thought it was probably a bad time and didn't want to bother me. If you are proactive with the habits I have laid out in this chapter, you don't have to worry about "bothering" your adult children. If you pursue their *heart*, they will recognize and welcome your efforts and not feel like you're trying to "fix" them. As a business owner, husband, and father of seven children, I can relate with your children. It is difficult to unplug. If, however, the reason you want to talk to your children is *to talk about them* and be a more caring and active mentor, you are pursing for the right reason. Never stop pursuing your children's hearts. It will be a journey that will add joy, peace, and a sense of purpose to this season of life.

Step Seven

PRACTICE LEISURE

"The first principle of all action is leisure.
Both are required, but leisure is better
than occupation and is its end."
—ARISTOTLE, *POLITICS*

When Angela and I landed in Rome for our honeymoon, we couldn't wait to grab our bags and start the adventure. We brought our wedding attire because our bishop back home had arranged for us to receive a blessing from Pope John Paul II, but you had to be dressed in wedding attire. Two by two, each pair of newlyweds were led up to a kneeler in front of the pope to receive a blessing. The moment and the picture are still hard to believe. The following day, a friend introduced us to then-Cardinal Joseph Ratzinger (who later was elected Pope Benedict XVI) to receive a marriage blessing. Little did we know, our honeymoon would include a blessing from two popes!

While waiting our turn to approach Pope John Paul II with about fifty other newly-married couples from around the world, we met another bride and groom from Louisiana. After the event was over, we decided to not waste time going back to the hotel room to change and instead spent the day touring in wedding attire with our new friends. It was a magical day. We received applause, cheers, and free food everywhere we went. By the end of the day, the bottom third of Angela's dress was brown from the dirty Italian roads we had walked all day.

Our hotel was tucked away into a little Italian neighborhood. We changed for dinner and then ended up dining at a local restaurant on a small square with a beautiful fountain. As we enjoyed our meal sitting in the courtyard, some neighborhood families walked into the square and started playing music. A few minutes later, there was singing and dancing—the joy in the air was spectacular. I remember the first thing that went through my mind was, "This is living." Then the second thing that went through my head was, "Wait a second, it's 9:00 p.m. on a Wednesday night; don't these people have school and work in the morning?"

I was shocked at how these Italians were celebrating life, and at the same time I was confused. Earlier that day, Angela and I were walking the streets of Rome carefree, but that's what we were supposed to be doing. We were on our honeymoon. We were on vacation; we were allowed to celebrate life. These people were singing and dancing in the street for no apparent reason—on a weeknight! This experience confused me, because I knew that weekdays were for work. Weekends were where you squeezed in a little fun, or at least recovered from a long week. These Italians did things differently. *Leisure* seemed to take priority. Retirees have more time for leisure, and they need to teach Generation 2 and 3 to have it too.

WHAT IS LEISURE?

Perhaps the best reflection on the meaning of leisure is a little book by the German philosopher Josef Pieper, called *Leisure, the Basis of Culture*. The book is a combination of two shorter essays written in 1947, "Leisure and Worship," and "The Philosophical Act." These two essays were published together in in 1952. The book was introduced by T.S. Eliot and gained considerable attention from reviewers such as the *New Statesman*, *The Nation*, the *Chicago Tribune*, the *San Francisco Chronicle*, and the *New York Times*. I am not sure why it received so much attention, but one can argue that over the last sixty years we have ventured quite far from understanding and practicing true leisure.

One way to understand leisure is by first understanding what *it is not*. In his book, Pieper explains leisure as different from the world of work.[30] Leisure and the "world of work" are two different vantage points from which one views himself and the world. One's focus and decision making either revolve around leisure or work. He proposes that if not properly ordered, the world of work leads to slavery while a life lived with leisure as its end will make a person more fully human. Leisure is a "non-productive" activity that is proper to human beings alone. Animals eat and sleep, and machines produce widgets, but only human beings can, for example, wonder at the stars.

So what does a person who views life from the "world of work" look like? Well, a typical week looks something like 1) work, 2) recover from work through entertainment and "vegging out," and 3) go back to work. *Work is the end*. Everything revolves around it, and all extra time, mind share, and energy is spent either *recovering from it* or *preparing for it*. This does not mean that earning a living and attending to our

---

30 Josef Peiper, *Leisure: The Basis of Culture* (Pantheon, 1963, reprinted 2009) p. 48.

practical needs is bad, and that is not what Pieper is referring to when he says the "world of work." He is not referring to work as such, but rather work as the vantage point, the basis, the axis that life revolves around. When the world of work is the basis of our life and culture, we are more concerned with micromanaging the supply and demand of all resources than we are with *getting back to leisure.* Even reading this book requires you to be at leisure. It is nonproductive but active—it isn't entertainment. It is being receptive to reality without the need to analyze, calculate, produce, or check something off the to-do list. It is the Italians singing and dancing in the street on a Wednesday night.

I know this is an in-depth, philosophical topic to tackle, but I believe you are in a unique season of life to not only understand it but to live it and build a culture of leisure within your family. I have noticed that most retirees, whether they consciously reflect on the concept of leisure or not, are in one of two groups. They are either fighting the world of work and intentionally trying to make time for leisure or they have substituted their job for some other busyness that is keeping them from being at leisure.

THE WORK VOID

The topic of being at leisure is a challenging one. It is difficult for almost everyone in today's culture, and retirement doesn't make leisure an instant habit. What retirement does do, however, is place leisure a bit more within your reach. In a way, you are now part of the "leisure class." Your income is secure, so you can turn your attention to higher, leisurely concerns. This sounds attractive, but I find that most retirees are just as busy, if not busier, than they were when they were working. I often hear a retiree explain, "I don't know how I got anything done when I worked. I am retired now, and I can barely keep up!"

The transition from working to retirement is something that shouldn't be taken lightly. I have witnessed numerous retirees struggle at first with the "work void" until eventually they surrender. If you were "productive" for thirty, forty, or fifty years, it can be hard to kick back and sit on your porch all day. Being active in retirement isn't a bad thing. Again, what we are discussing in this chapter is building a culture of leisure—not laziness. The idea is to set an example in your family that it is good to be active yet not productive. I know that sounds "inefficient," but it is a wonderful role to play in your family. You may be the only one who sees the importance of living like a human being rather than a machine. Sometimes it is difficult to see the whole wheel turning when you are just a cog. At this stage in life, you have a better vantage point than your heirs.

The other day, I walked in my house during lunch, and initially I didn't see anyone. I didn't see little people running around, but there were signs everywhere I looked. As I walked in the front door, I noticed the ottomans in the living room tipped over and toys scattered about. I walked down the hallway and stepped over the broom and dustpan lying next to a pile of crumbs—a pile that was losing its form thanks to little feet having trouble missing it. Then as I walked through the kitchen, I noticed the sink full to the brim with dishes. At this point, my neat-nick side began to bubble up and I prepared to share my frustration with the first person I encountered. I entered the "schoolroom," and Angela was sitting on the couch reading Howard Pyle's *Robin Hood* aloud while all the children sat at the table coloring peacefully listening to the story. It was a beautiful sight to behold.

I know if I were the one who had the responsibility of homeschooling our children, they wouldn't learn very much...but the house would be clean. When I read and reflect on the story in Luke's gospel about Martha and Mary—Martha keeping busy while

Mary sits at Jesus' feet—I know I am Martha. [31] My wife, thank God, is Mary; always fully present and always focused on the most important things. Her disposition and personality tends towards leisure, recognizing and living goodness, while mine tends towards the "world of work," staying in control or producing measurable results. It is important to recognize where you fall.

If you no longer have a day job, I encourage you to make time for leisure and share that experience with your children. It is possible to be busier in retirement than when you were working, but resist. Sign up for art lessons, learn to dance, read a book with a friend, go fishing with your grandson but only take one pole (he focuses on fishing while you focus on him). Fill your day spending time with those you love and non-productive activity—activity that is good for your soul. Your family needs to witness you at leisure, because they probably don't see it anywhere else.

SCREEN TIME

If you like the idea of living a more leisurely life as well as encouraging leisure in your family, the biggest obstacle you may encounter is a little computer that fits in your pocket. What does this have to do with

---

31 Luke 10:38-42

building a culture of leisure in your family? This may seem radical, but I believe that "screen time" might be the biggest obstacle you will face when trying to live a life of leisure and share that sort of life with your family. The "virtual world" as we know it has begun to take priority over the real world. For some, this virtual world feels more real. The thing about leisure is that it requires an "unplugging" from the virtual in order to encounter the real.

The author, poet, and Pulitzer Prize winner Carl Sandburg was friends with the president of Zenith Corporation. One year, his friend gave him one of the first remote-controlled televisions. I am sure he was thankful, but he probably didn't watch it much. He was known to tell family and friends (especially younger family members) that "TV is the thief of time." I think nowadays, most people would agree that a smartphone, Facebook, Netflix, and many other apps and technological devices are a thief of time. Not only are they a thief of time, but they may be doing us just as much harm as good.

A recent study conducted by the University of Texas found that the mere presence of a smartphone reduces cognitive ability. The authors of the study conducted experiments with nearly 800 smartphone users. Participants were asked to take a series of computer-based tests that required full concentration. Before beginning, they were asked to shut off their phone and either place it in a locker outside the room, in their pocket, or face down on the desk. Those who chose to leave their phone outside of the testing room scored higher on the tests, while those who had their phone near them, whether in their pocket or on the desk, did worse. The mere presence of a smartphone (even though it was turned off) reduced their cognitive capacity.[32] Perhaps we should rethink the term "smartphone."

A few years ago, I was thinking about this topic as my daughter's baptism approached. Angela and I had family from both sides coming into town for the celebration. Now, before I explain what happened, let me first say that I own a smartphone, and I struggle with everything I am writing about in this chapter. If I am honest, this is an area of my life where I must set boundaries to make sure I am always present to those around me. As the baptism drew near, I knew there was a chance that when we returned to the house for the reception there would be many phones in hands that would put a damper on conversation and celebration. One of my biggest pet peeves is

---

32   Adrian F. Ward, et. al, "Brain Drain: The Mere Presence of One's Own Smartphone Reduces Available Cognitive Capacity," *Association for Consumer Research* vol. 2 no. 2, (April, 2017).

watching one of my children try to speak to an adult and the adult not respond because they are looking at their phone.

After the baptism concluded and everyone was standing outside the church, I made the announcement that we would gather at our home for a little celebration. I also made the announcement that our home would be a "cell phone free zone" and, if possible, please leave your phone in your car. It remained a little quiet after the announcement. I don't think anyone minded, but they were a little shocked that I made the request.

One and all accepted, with my request, and we had a wonderful afternoon. Everyone was fully present with one another, and distractions were at a minimum. Our children and their cousins put on a play, and everyone watched attentively without disruption. It reminded me of being a kid sitting on the floor in my great Aunt Betty's living room. After dinner, all the adults would sit and talk while they ate pie and drank coffee. No phones, no computers—just real-life people sharing real-life moments.

If you want to live a more leisurely life and introduce the habit to your heirs, I encourage you to be bold in this area. Side comments won't do the trick. If you host your children and grandchildren at your house or take them on a trip, make clear requests about limiting screen time. These moments are precious, and if not protected, they will be stolen away by an unexpected "thief of time."

A LEISURELY IDEA

Limiting screen time may reduce one obstacle to leisure, but it won't make it automatic. Hopefully, you have a "Mary" in your life that you can turn to as an example of leisure. Fortunately, I have my wife to set the example for me, and my oldest daughter, Ava, is following in her footsteps. It is a wonderful blessing to watch your children grow up. As their personality forms, it is neat to witness the uniqueness of every child. Ava *lives* for leisure. She is studious, does her chores, and completes the various jobs that are required of her as the oldest of six younger siblings, but her mind and heart are always longing to *get back to leisure*. From the window of my home office, I often see her laying on the hammock beneath the Japanese maple, enthralled in a good book. When we get home from a Saturday afternoon of running errands, she grabs her knitting kit while everyone else is ready to lay on the couch and watch a movie. She writes two or three letters a week to friends and family members. For Ava, life is about getting the necessary tasks completed so she can get back to *higher things.*

One night several years ago, I was sitting on the couch watching Ava practice her cursive in her long-hand workbook. I asked to see it and it brought back memories of learning long-hand in grade school—an art I had long since forgotten. It reminded me of the letters my grandfather had written to my grandmother when he was at sea during World War II. Those were his words, and *that was his handwriting.* These thoughts created a desire within me to re-teach myself long-hand. I made a copy of Ava's workbook— the page that shows every uppercase and lowercase letter—and I began to practice my cursive with every note I wrote. This was an arduous and frustrating exercise, but after hundreds of ripped-up notecards, I am proud to say I have officially re-taught myself how to write in cursive. Following Ava's letter-writing example, I now write each of my children a letter every Christmas. I hope the words will be a source of love and affirmation for them for many years to come.

I invite you to start writing to your children. The practice of writing is a great way to start developing a culture of leisure in your family. I know for me it isn't the easiest item on my to-do list—it is hard to unplug, reflect, and commit the time to a hand-written letter, but that is good. It is good to add this sort of practice into your regular routine, because it will force you to be at leisure—or perhaps reveal to you how far you are from it. It is easy to send a text or Facebook message to a loved one, but writing a letter requires much more. It is a practical way to communicate to your heirs that taking time (away from screens), and connecting with family is important. Your children will be on the receiving end of these letters, and hopefully they will follow your example. And before you know it, you will have begun to create a culture of leisure in your family.

CONCLUSION

——

I hope you have enjoyed reading *The Great Inheritance*. When I read books like this, the concepts are enlightening, but I often feel a bit overwhelmed. If you found the content helpful but you don't know where to start, this chapter will help. In the following pages, I have laid out ideas to give you a jump-start on implementing the seven steps of this book. We are creatures of habit, and it is just as hard to break bad habits as it is to start new ones. I encourage you to begin by tackling one or two of the steps that come to you most naturally. If you begin by implementing ideas that come easier to you, you have a better chance of continuing the process. If you are like me and you need baby steps, below are a few ideas to get you going.

SEVEN STEPS QUICK-START GUIDE
STEP ONE: CAPTURE YOUR STORY

This step provided a list of questions you can consider and journal with to help you record your family story. If that list seems daunting, an easier way to get started might be to write down three character traits that are most important to you. Once you have completed that, write down one family member for each of the character traits—a family member who you believe exemplifies that character trait. Now, try to recall a moment when you witnessed this person exercise the specific character trait listed. Perhaps you witnessed your grandfather help someone in need or your mom work nights to provide for your family. This should help unearth some stories that you can record for future generations. It may also help to recall experiences in your own life that you would like future generations to know about.

This method might be easier than trying to come up with illustrations from thin air. Just keep it simple. (1. What's important? 2. Who lived it? 3. When did I witness it?) It will help jog your memory and may lead to all sorts of experiences that you will want to capture. I've found once this ball gets rolling, it's hard to know where to stop!

STEP TWO: RESTORE AND STRENGTHEN FAMILY BONDS

I proposed in this step that, as the leader in your family, you should initiate reconciliation by being the first to ask for forgiveness. Finding the "plank" in your own eye and initially only focusing on that— whether your fault in a conflict is 90 percent or 10 percent, start with you. I admit this is a challenging suggestion, but I have only experienced fruit from doing it myself.

If there are long-standing or deep fractures in your family, it may be hard to even contemplate engaging—especially if your children have made extremely poor choices and hold most of the blame. If this is the case, I encourage you to start with *one specific item*, no matter how small, and ask forgiveness. If you reflect on the relationship long enough, I am sure you can find at least one act or omission that you can ask forgiveness for.

Once you have identified it, write out what you are going to say—and be specific so they know you are sincere. This will help ensure that emotion doesn't take over and that your focus remains on your fault. I have had clients write a letter and others make a phone call. If this is the first time you have engaged your heir in this way, it may take them by surprise.

Don't let the conversation go down rabbit holes. If your heir starts to express the pain associated with the item you are addressing, let them be heard, and ask them for forgiveness.

If you are going to use this method, make sure you are prepared to have the conversation without reverting to a defensive posture or focusing on your own justification. Remember, the most important aspect of restoring and strengthening family bonds is working on you more than anyone else. If you take the lead in this step from a place of humility, it will bear greater fruit than all the other steps combined.

STEP THREE: DESIGN AN ORDERLY ESTATE

This step covered a lot of information, from risk tolerance to taxes to estate planning. The most important thing you can do right off the bat is answer the questions I provided for determining whether or not you are working with a *retirement specialist*. I have listed the questions here again for your convenience:

1. Do you have a detailed distribution plan in place that projects all your streams of income from now until age 100?
2. Do you have a spousal continuation plan in place

that details how a surviving spouse will make up lost income due to the first spouse passing?

3. Do you have a summary of assets in place that lists all your assets, the taxable nature of those assets, and who the beneficiary is?

4. Do you know your risk tolerance (more specifically, your *Risk Number*) and the amount you could lose if you experienced a market correction or crash?

5. Has your advisor spoken with your attorney to make sure that you have all your necessary legal documents in place?

6. Does your advisor meet with your CPA or accountant to make sure your estate is structured as tax-efficiently as possible?

7. Has your advisor spoken with you about long-term care? Not necessarily offered you a product to purchase, but asked you what your desires are for your care?

8. Has your advisor offered to meet with your heirs and explain in detail how your estate is structured and help prepare the person you have appointed to lead the wealth transfer process?

9. Has your advisor classified your assets into the three Tax Buckets and suggested strategies for transferring assets into the Tax-Free Bucket?

10. Does your advisor meet with you at least annually to review the above areas and adjust your plan according to your goals or changes in your life?

If you answer "No" to any of them, it may be time to look for another advisor. But not just any advisor, someone who 1) is held to the fiduciary standard, 2) works for an independent firm, and 3) specifically focuses on serving retirees. If you would like help finding a financial advisor who meets these criteria, visit www.jbiance.com, or call (863) 304-8959 and we will help you find someone in your area.

STEP FOUR: ENLIGHTEN HEIRS AND FIDUCIARIES

Most retirees prefer to keep the details of their assets private. This is understandable for several reasons. This step encourages you to keep what you own private, but not to keep roles and expectations private. To get started with this step, you simply have to put one of two meetings on the calendar. If you don't currently have your estate plan drafted and up to date, you need to schedule a meeting with your attorney. If you are wondering what documents you should have completed, they are:

- Last Will & Testament
- Durable General Power of Attorney
- Living Will and Health Care Surrogate
- Revocable Living Trust (if needed)

If you have these documents and they are consistent

with your desires, you need to schedule a meeting with your heirs and fiduciaries. In most cases, gathering these folks together is not an easy task; therefore, just focus on getting it on the calendar.

You may think to yourself, "This will only take a phone call. I will just send them the documents and tell each of them the role they will play." This is tempting, but I strongly advise having a meeting with everyone in the same room. Everyone will have a chance to ask questions and hear answers in your presence and in the presence of their fellow heirs and fiduciaries. If there is doubt, confusion, or questions that arise (and they will), it is best that you provide an opportunity for them to surface while you are living. Take it one step at a time. Get the meeting on the calendar. If you get pushback from your children, just tell them you want to meet concerning their inheritance—it shouldn't take much arm-twisting to get them there.

STEP FIVE: CREATE A FAMILY CHARTER

If you successfully completed Step One: *Capture Your Story*, you are well on your way to creating a Family Charter. From the stories you recalled during that step, write down principles that you hope your family will live by for generations to come. To help you organize your thoughts, you can use these categories or others that may be a better fit for your family:

- Family & Relationships
- Work & Money
- Faith & Spirituality

Your final Family Charter can be a list of principles, or you can work it into more of a statement. I find that working a list of principles into a succinct statement usually requires a third party to help facilitate the process. Therefore, I encourage you to just record the principles that you hold dear—principles that are rooted in your story and that of your ancestors. Then when you have your meeting with your heirs (Step Four), you can present a simple Family Charter that reads, "The principles that we the [Last Name] Family hold dear are as follows..."

Memorializing your family principles by creating a Family Charter—even in a simplified format—is essential for passing on *who you* are along with *what you have*.

STEP SIX: BUILD A CULTURE OF MENTORSHIP

The quickest path to building a culture of mentorship is giving sufficient time to Step Two: *Restore and*

Strengthen Family Bonds. It is difficult to engage in mentoring if there is not mutual trust and friendship. Along with that, there are two main practices that will help you mature into a mentoring relationship with your children.

The first practice is what I call "one-sided conversations." The next time you call or visit your child (or other mentee), try to keep the conversation about *them* 100 percent of the time. Mentors can tend towards the "know-it-all" posture, and this little practice helps prevent that. The problem with a know-it-all mentor is that a mentee picks up on it immediately and knows you are not in it for them. If you call your child and are more focused on *sounding interesting* than *being interested* in them, they will be less open and receptive in the relationship.

The second practice is to treat your children as fellow adults, not older kids. Your relationship with them has changed, and while I know there are problems today with immaturity, it is best to speak and act toward an adult as an adult, even your kids. This means respecting their authority in their own lives and their decisions, not because they are the right decisions but because they are the right one to make the decision. In mentoring, you don't direct every thought and act of another, but you earn the right to be heard through respecting the person and the place they're in. It is belittling to have parents treat you as a child when you are, in fact, an adult. Be a loving friend that has wisdom when asked, not the unwanted coach that force-feeds advice.

STEP SEVEN: PRACTICE LEISURE

This final step may be the most difficult, but it also may be the easiest to start. If you don't already practice some sort of leisure in your life (a non-productive but important activity) it is perhaps because you are too busy being productive. Another enemy of leisure is stimulation. Whether it is the television or a smartphone, screens not only consume time, but they also make leisure less attractive. It is sort of like eating out versus having a healthy, home-cooked meal. If you eat out a lot of the time and then have a rare, home-cooked meal, it isn't salty enough, isn't sweet enough—it's just not as exciting to the taste buds. In fact, the food seems almost tasteless because of the regular dose of salt and sugar you are used to at restaurants. The same is true of leisure. Too much productivity makes *being at rest* extremely difficult, and too much screen time makes leisure unattractive.

Therefore, the best place to start when it comes to leisure is *making room* for it. Productivity or stimulation consume our days, so begin by reducing one of them and surrendering that time to leisure. For example, if you are used to watching the news after dinner, take the first thirty minutes to read before turning on the television. Or perhaps you wake up every morning ready to attack your to-do list. Pick a day (or half a day) that you commit to do nothing on it. Take a walk, write a letter, or invite someone over for tea. Sometimes it is hard not to be *productive* all the time, but you can do it if you try.

As I explained in the introduction, most families (70–90 percent) do not experience successful wealth transfers, and the greatest cause is not financial or legal instruments. It is the communication with and preparedness of heirs.[33] Assets aren't surviving two generations, but the greater failure is not passing on family stories, principles, and unity. While preserving your wealth for multiple generations is a worthwhile goal, research tells us that making these non-financial issues your priority is the best strategy.

A GREAT INHERITANCE

My goal in writing this book is that it would contain what you need to pass on more than your money. If

---

33 Roy Williams and Vic Preisser, *Preparing Heirs* (San Francisco: Robert Reed Publishers, 2010).

the steps and this quick-start guide leave you eager to start but still in need of some guidance, you can visit www.jbiance.com. There, you can learn more about Inheritance Design, our personalized consulting service.

It is my hope that you and your family will be blessed by this book. My prayer is that your great-great-grandchildren will receive *who you are* along with what you have. It's worth the work, because what you have to offer truly is a *Great Inheritance.*

ABOUT THE AUTHOR

JUSTIN BIANCE is a Certified Estate Planner® specializing in multigenerational legacy planning. His wealth management firm, J. Biance Financial (www. jbiance.com), has offices in Florida and North Carolina. Justin is the creator of Inheritance Design, a planning program that helps retirees memorialize their family vision and prepare their heirs for their inheritance. He has an MS in Entrepreneurship from the University of Florida, an MA in Moral Theology from Holy Apostles College and Seminary, and is founder of the mentoring organization Fraternus Inc. (www.Fraternus.net). He and his wife Angela have seven children and live in western North Carolina.

www.ingramcontent.com/pod-product-compliance
Lightning Source LLC
Chambersburg PA
CBHW031500180326
41458CB00044B/6652/J